THE YORKSHIRE MARY ROSE

The Ship *General Carleton* of Whitby

by

STEPHEN BAINES

BLACKTHORN PRESS

Blackthorn Press, Blackthorn House
Middleton Rd, Pickering YO18 8AL
United Kingdom

www.blackthornpress.com

ISBN 978 1 906259 20 4

Printed and bound in Great Britain by
CPI Antony Rowe, Chippenham and Eastbourne

Dedicated to Dr Waldemar Ossowski, without whom nothing.

And in memory of Harold Brown and Syd Barnett, two wonderful men who loved Whitby and who worked tirelessly and selflessly at the Whitby 'Lit & Phil'.

Contents

Introduction

Why is *General Carleton* so Important?

The excavation of the wreck of *General Carleton* is of enormous and international significance, for four reasons.

Firstly, she is a merchant ship. The Royal Navy warships in the Age of Sail have dominated the attention and the publicity. But around the time when *General Carleton* was built in 1777 there were some 81,000 British owned ships, of which 416 (5%) belonged to the Royal Navy, and of these only 270 (3.3%) were ships-of-the-line. It is good that in recent decades there has been a real focus among academics and underwater archaeologists on the other 95% of British shipping, and the vital role it has played in increasing trade and providing crucial support to both army and navy. Important examples in recent decades have been the Bermuda wreck, Dr Kathy Abbass' on-going research on the transports sunk in Newport harbour in 1778, Dr John Broadwater's work on the vessels sunk in 1780 at the Siege of Yorktown, and Waldemar Ossowski's excavation of *General Carleton* which sank in 1785.

Secondly, we know which ship she is. The sea floor is littered with shipwrecks of trading vessels. A fraction of those are excavated, and of those a fraction can be clearly identified. Clever reading of relevant documents enabled Dr Broadwater to identify a Yorktown ship as *Betsy* of Whitehaven, Younghusband as master. This was impressive deduction, as the ship had been scuttled and nearly all the contents had been removed, so the evidence was fairly scanty. With *General Carleton* one of the first items brought up from the wreck was the ship's bell, with the clear inscription: GENERAL CARLETON OF WHITBY 1777 which enabled the wreck to be identified quickly and certainly. Once identified, the ship could be linked with relevant contemporary paperwork. Her story is fairly clear, at least in outline, and we know the names of all those mariners who sailed on her.

Thirdly, The wreck yielded a great number of artefacts in a good state of preservation. The pine tar in the cargo, mixing with sand and Baltic seawater, created a matrix which covered many of the articles, preserving items which would not otherwise have survived. Particularly notable is the uniquely large collection of seamen's clothing, which has been described by Professor Lawrence Babits as: *the finest collection of well-dated 18th-century common male's clothing ever found*. It is the profusion of artefacts, ranging from the nautical to the personal, which gives us such insight into the lives of ordinary sailors of the period and has caused *General Carleton* to be termed *The Yorkshire 'Mary Rose'*.

And finally, the muster rolls revealed the exact date when *General Carleton* sank. This provided a very specific *terminus ad quem* for the artefacts, which is of great help to scholars when dating similar objects discovered on other archaeological sites.

Though it is the product of countless hours of research, this is not an academic book; it is a story book. It is the story of a ship which was wrecked when it was only eight years old, the story of those associated directly or indirectly with that ship, and the story of Whitby and its environs at a time when it was significantly involved in some of the crucial events of British history.

Although *General Carleton* is now of exceptional importance, at the time there was nothing very special about her. She was similar to many other contemporary merchant vessels, and so this story is also, in a way, about those numerous unknown other merchant sailing ships, brigs, barks, schooners and brigantines and about the innumerable men (and women) who sailed on them – so many of whom are part of the *unhonour'd dead* who *have no memorial* but who, nonetheless, helped to shape our history and are our ancestors.

Stephen Baines

Chapter 1

September 1785
Shipwreck

1785 was a good year politically. England had been at war with the American colonists, the French, the Dutch and the Spanish in a long war which had ended in 1783, and was now enjoying peace. Although trade was picking up after the war and the seas were safer, the sudden flooding of the labour market with thousands of discharged soldiers and sailors had resulted in a catastrophic unemployment, and a slump in seamen's wages. The American War of Independence had involved numerous Government contracts for transport ships, victualling ships and storeships; but that lucrative source of income for shipowners had dried up. Although the country's economy was booming, there were too many ships and too many sailors, and the atmosphere in the merchant marine was of gloom and economic uncertainty.

Such thoughts were in the mind of William Hustler, master of the Whitby ship *General Carleton*, as she left the port of Stockholm, laden with iron and pine tar bound for London. Sweden produced iron in abundance, but used very little, whereas England's growing industrialisation, and massive shipbuilding industry had created a ready market for iron. It looked as if it was going to be a profitable voyage, which would make the owners happy. Keeping the owners happy was important, as no-one's job was safe in the current economic climate. William Hustler was getting on; he was 47, with a small 10-year-old son and an impoverished widowed mother at home to support. The death of his father at a comparatively early age had left William the only breadwinner in the family; he had had to support his two sisters, and provide them with a dowry, but now they were both married, so his financial prospects were looking better. His aim was to save sufficient money to buy a part-share of several ships, so that he could retire and live off their profits, and would no longer have to face the dangers of the sea, or the humiliation of struggling to find a post on a ship when he became too old to do it effectively. He thought that perhaps ten years, maybe less, working as master mariner would provide him with the requisite financial solidarity. He should be able to last that long, he thought, though he was already becoming very long-sighted and needed magnifying glasses to be able to see the detail on his navigational charts.

One of the perks of being a captain, was that you could carry a small personal cargo (*deck cargo*) for your own commercial benefit. William had purchased some fine pewter buckles in the modern style which polished up to be as shiny as silver, and which he hoped would sell at a good profit in London.

The passage out into the Baltic from Stockholm could be tricky, though he had done it before. A pilot would ensure the ship reached Dallero or Sandham, but he was then on his own to reach Landsort and the open sea.

But 1785 was a bad year for weather. Winds and rain had ravaged most of northern Europe, and the gossip in Stockholm had been that further inclement weather was on the way, which would threaten the harvest and raise the price of bread. William was more concerned about sailing home safely: although the weather in the Baltic had been particularly mild for September so far, the suddenness and violence of Baltic storms was legendary, and the North Sea had also been the graveyard of many mariners. He had confidence in his crew. Although he had had a different mate for each of the four years he

1

had been master of *General Carleton*, the present one, John Swan, had served as 2nd mate the previous year and had shown he could do the job well, and William thought he would make master soon. John Pearson, the carpenter, was also new that year, but had come highly recommended, and in the five months he had been aboard he had demonstrated skill and competence. William was also pleased with the efficiency of the six sailors he had signed on in July: one of the advantages of there being a glut of sailors for hire in London, was that you could be more selective about whom you hired. Some of the apprentices were also shaping up well: James Hart, John Thompson and John Noble were in their fourth year on *General Carleton*, starting when William took over as master from Thomas Pyman; John Fraiser and Richard Neale were in their third. John Johnson and Richard Trueman had started together in 1779, when *General Carleton* was only two years old, and so were in the last year of their apprenticeship; next season they would sail as seaman or second mate, and would then probably move on to being mate shortly after; William thought that they might be masters in their turn by 1790.

    General Carleton had not been long out from the archipelago into the Baltic when the weather deteriorated. The skies darkened, the rain began to pour down, and the north-easterly wind freshened, threatening a gale. William made suitable preparations, his orders being given to Swan who ensured they were carried out: all hands were called on deck, the topsails were furled, and the topgallant masts and yards lowered to the deck; the wheel was double-manned, everything moveable on deck was taken below or securely fastened, the boat was covered with canvas, lifelines were rigged, and a tarpaulin weather cloth was spread in the mizzen rigging to provide some cover. The ship was readied for scudding before the wind, with just a single sail on the foremast to provide some manoeuvrability. William ensured that John Noble, a young but sufficiently experienced apprentice, was near him ready to run with orders which would not be heard above the noise of the impending storm, and to bring back information.

    John Pearson, the carpenter, would ensure the mast wedges were not loose, check the pumps were in working order, batten down the hatches[1], and ensure the materials were at hand to caulk leaks.

    The storm then struck in its full force, the rain turning to swirling snow and then to hail. *General Carleton* was driven before the wind, the crew doing their best to ensure the sandglass was turned when empty and the bell rung every half hour, the logline would be thrown out regularly and the speed checked. It was crucial to have as good an idea as possible as to where the ship was, even though William found it was impossible to get an accurate reading with his sextant for the noon sighting, because the sun was obscured by grey clouds, and because of the violent motion of the ship as she was thrown about on the waves. Perilously secured at the bow of the ship, Andrew Gibson was taking regular soundings, with John Noble waiting to relay the information back to the captain.

    The ship had passed between Gotland and Öland safely, but she was taking a real beating, and was leaking badly, in spite of the two sea pumps being constantly manned, and the best efforts of John Pearson. As *General Carleton* was not only shipping water, but also – as a consequence – listing badly and difficult to control, Hustler thought the best plan was to attempt to reach Danzig (Gdańsk), where the ship could find shelter, and be properly repaired.

---

[1] This process involved putting a tarpaulin over the hatchway, which would be secured by hammering battens round the edges. A corner would be left open on one of the hatchways to ensure emergency access.

Fig 1: *General Carleton* **scudding before the gale.**

They were now sailing south into what William had hoped was Danzig Bay. The soundsman's cry from the bow was "By the mark, five!" followed shortly after by "Sand!" The voice was lost in the shrieking of the wind, but the attentive John Noble heard and struggled aft, clutching the lifeline and already soaked through with the gigantic waves that would suddenly splash over the deck. He was almost out of breath when he reported to William Hustler on the quarter-deck, "Five fathoms, sir, pure sand". The Master acknowledged the information, and Noble went forward once more.

His hands were frozen, and he regretted not wearing the woollen gloves which were stowed in his sea-chest; but sailors were expected to be bare-handed: gloves could get caught in the ropes and pulleys and cause serious accidents. Even Andrew Gibson wore no gloves as he skilfully swung the lead out beyond the bow of the ship at just the right distance to ensure that it was firmly grounded with the leadline taut at the very moment the ship passed over it. His fingers were so numb that the only way he could recognise the marks was by touching them to his lips; it was his tongue that had recognised the cotton rag. Again the lead was heaved.

"And a half, four!" John Noble set out once more.

Hustler knew that he would be sailing over sand, and five fathoms was a good depth. He was beginning to feel more hopeful, maybe they could keep the ship afloat until they reached Danzig. Then he saw the form of young John Noble, indistinct and grey in the

1: Stockholm. The modern harbour frontage would have been recognisable to William Hustler.

2: Some of William Hustler's deck cargo of buckles.

3: The pumps which would have been used to attempt to keep *General Carleton* afloat.

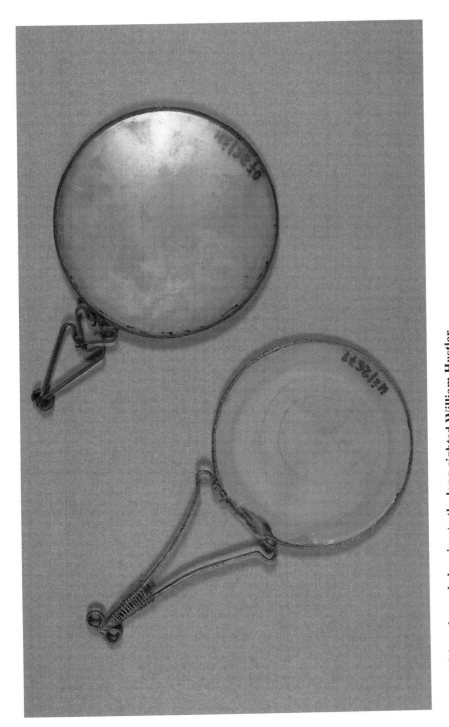

4: Magnifying glasses belonging to the long-sighted William Hustler.

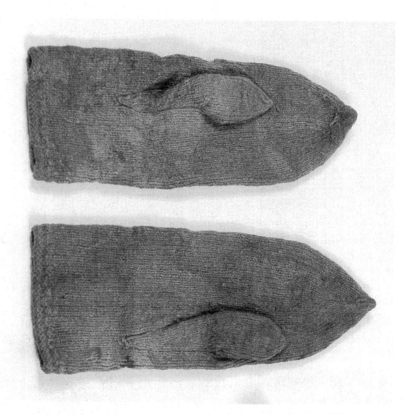

5: Hand-knitted woollen mittens, which closely resemble traditional Latvian mittens, and so may have been purchased in Riga.

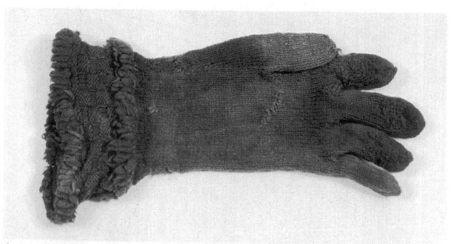

6: A technically rather elaborate woollen glove. Its many repairs suggest it has been well-used in rough work; perhaps someone was wearing gloves when they should not have been.

7: Underwater picture showing the timber framework of *General Carleton*.

8: Underwater picture of one of *General Carleton*'s anchors.

swirling rain, struggling to reach him. Clutching the rail he reached the quarter-deck; shivering with cold he stammered out, "F-four and a half fathoms, sir!"

It was perhaps then that Hustler realised that far from sailing down to Danzig, the ship was being driven on a sandy lee shore on the northern coast. It was a time for quick decisions; on a gently sloping sandy shore it would be possible to beach the ship – Whitby ships, like *General Carleton* and James Cook's *Endeavour* (which she so closely resembled), were built with almost flat bottoms so they could easily be run onto a sandy beach. There were dangers in that a strong hind-wind would drive the vessel on the beach with too great a speed and fury which may cause the ship to keel over or more probably, in its rather fragile condition, to break up. But it would have possibly been the best option had the sea bottom been gently sloping; however this was not the case. Conditions in that part of the Baltic Sea caused steep ridges of sand to form horizontally to the shore (as is the case to this day). Once Hustler realised where he was, he may have been aware of this feature of this coast, or he may have looked towards the coast and have seen the waves breaking on the outermost of the sandbanks, and realised that if the ship struck it, she would certainly founder and, in the prevailing storm, be wrecked.

"By the deep, four!"

Quickly the order was given to lower the best bower anchor; the ship was turned into the wind, the foresail was taken in and the anchor dropped. The *General Carleton* came to rest with its bow now to the north, held by the anchor. This prevented the ship from being driven ashore, and also gave William Hustler time to think. As the gale was still blowing, he really had no option but to hope for the best: the motion of the ship's riding the waves while at anchor would alternately loosen the cable and then stretch it, putting a strain not only on the cable itself but also on the structure of the ship – already weakened by the constant battering of the storm since they left Stockholm. There was no way with an onshore wind (a lee shore) that *General Carleton* was going to sail out to sea until the gale stopped, but if she didn't there was a danger that either the anchor-cable would break, or the tugging motion of the cable would pull the ship apart: in either case *General Carleton* would be blown, stern-first and uncontrollably, towards the coast.

The coast was only some 450 yards away, and William Hustler, through his telescope, could see the small fishing village of Dębki, with its colourful boats drawn up high on the shore, and the estuary of the small river Piasnica meandering its way across the sandy beach. As the storm had abated somewhat he gave the commands to lower the boat, and for the members of the crew to make for the shore and save themselves if possible, with instructions to return the next day if the storm had subsided and if the ship was still afloat. He asked for a volunteer to help him save the ship, and Nicholas Theaker had stepped forward, encouraged by the reward which was offered. The other 16 members of the crew clambered down into the boat which proved difficult to control in the heavy sea, with the waves throwing it about and washing over it as the crew struggled for the safety of the land. In the event all the crew seem to have reached the shore[2].

Hustler, true to his obligation, stayed with the ship and the cargo while there was the slightest chance of it being saved. It was the safe delivery of the cargo that paid for their wages. The storm did subside and gave some moments of comparative tranquillity, while the two men took it in turns to operate the pump in an attempt to keep the creaking, leaking and

---

[2] See Appendix Three: How many people died in the *General Carleton* Shipwreck?

badly damaged ship afloat. Then a new storm, blowing now from north north-west, struck *General Carleton* with a sudden fury, smashing one of the masts which crashed over the side in a tangle of rope and canvas. Then as afternoon darkened into evening the anchor cable finally broke and the ship was driven onto the submerged sandbank. The port side of her stern section was smashed open and the water poured in, and, weighted down by her freight of Swedish iron, she sank into the sandy seafloor.

According to local legend, the crew were looked after by the local fishermen, who fed them and gave them a meal, and brought them wine and vodka. At first light they must all have made for the shore to see nothing of their ship except her masts above the water, and the shoreline covered in a jetsam of wooden spars and small objects. Among this debris might have been the bodies of William Hustler and Nicholas Theaker, the only two members of the crew who were known to have died. If this was the case they would have been buried ashore with minimal ceremony before the sailors and the local inhabitants set out to the wreck to salvage what they could that would be useful or saleable.

Details of the wreck filtered back to Britain; it was not until 21 October that *Lloyds List* reported that *General Carleton* was totally lost in the Baltic. The same account mentioned there being only three survivors, possibly a considerable understatement.

As the ship sank into the sea, the wind and waves would have wrought their damage: sweeping the decks clear and taking away what remained of the rigging. Gradually she collapsed in on herself, no longer a ship but a wreck, and in time the sands covered what was left of her.

Chapter 2

1995 - 9
Excavation

On 5 September 1995 the research vessel *Kaszubski Brzeg* anchored off the north coast of Poland some 450 metres from Dębki (pronounced *Dembki*) beach, above the site of a shipwreck.

Dębki in summer is a flourishing tourist resort where thousands of visitors come to spend time on one of Poland's most beautiful beaches. In winter Dębki reverts to its traditional existence as a small rather isolated farming and fishing community of fewer than 200 inhabitants located where the brown peaty Piaśnica river meanders its way to the Baltic through woods of oak, pine and beech which are the home to wild boar. After work the villagers gather in front of a blazing log fire at the local café to chat and tell stories over a dish of traditional *pierogi* dumplings or a bowl of *żurek* soup, washed down with a glass of vodka. Or they may drink mugs of strong Polish-style unfiltered coffee.

One of the many tales told on such occasions, passed on through the generations, was of a British wooden sailing ship sailing to St Petersburg loaded with porcelain and treasure. Damaged in a storm, she anchored off Dębki and the crew went ashore where they were entertained by one of the local residents. During this party, after much vodka had been consumed, the sailors let slip that there were riches of some kind onboard. The host's grandfather rowed out to the abandoned ship and, in two trips, stole all the valuables which he could carry away and buried them in a secret place up-river. Returning later to collect his hoard, he could not remember where he had hidden it – and the treasure is still there to this day waiting for someone to find it…

There are obviously events in this story which seem unlikely: the master would have stayed on board to protect the cargo, and it is difficult to imagine how the grandfather could have climbed on board and (twice!) looted the ship which was being defended by at least one younger man who would have been armed. And buried treasure stories are the stuff of folk fiction.

Tales handed on orally suffer from two contradictory influences: one, sometimes called *The Three Little Pigs Effect*, is that the exact words of an often-repeated story will tend to become fixed and unchanging (*I'll huff and I'll puff and I'll **blow** your house down*) thus preserving the original; the other, sometimes called *The Chinese Whispers Effect*, is that in the re-telling a tale can be misheard, misunderstood and (either deliberately or subconsciously) altered – often by exaggeration or by improving the structure (*storifying*). Trying to discover the true elements in oral tradition is not unlike the conservation and preservation of an artefact recovered from the seabed after many years: it may be damaged, distorted and accreted but something of the real original object is still there in one form or another.

To discover the truth behind the legend of the Dębki shipwreck, Dr Michał Woźniewski, professional ichthyologist and amateur scuba diver, performed a systematic search of the seafloor and discovered the remains of a wooden vessel. Dr Woźniewski told The Polish Maritime Museum at Gdańsk, who catalogued the wreck as W-32, and designated their recently-appointed underwater archaeologist Dr Waldemar Ossowski to head a group to excavate the wreck. Which is why the Museum's research vessel was anchored above W-32 that summer morning in 1995.

Starting work excavating a new wreck is always exciting: a mixture of hopeful anticipation of interesting new discoveries and worry about the practical details and difficulties. There was a real adrenalin buzz among the team as they prepared for what was intended to be the first day of a month-long project; but at the time none of them could have known quite the extent and importance of the finds, nor the immense difficulties that this enterprise, which would stretch over more than two busy seasons, would entail.

At first things did not look good: a recent storm had stirred up the seabed so visibility was minimal and the divers, groping as if in a thick fog, could barely make out the wooden plankwork of the vessel's hull. Fortunately the water cleared and it was apparent that the turbulence of the sea had in fact moved a large amount of sand from around the wreck, revealing more of W-32's structure. Unlike most wrecks near the coast which are parallel to the shore, this wreck was oriented away from the shore with its bow pointing almost due north. Artefacts were soon discovered: an anchor to east of the ship and another some 300 metres to the north, and a firehearth, the stove on which the crew's meals would have been cooked, to the west. Then they found the ship's bell, which was clearly inscribed *GENERAL CARLETON OF WHITBY 1777*. At last, W-32 had a name.

None of the team had heard of Whitby. Interestingly, a sister ship of *Kaszubski Brzeg*, a fishing trawler called *Puszcyk*, also built in the North Gdańsk shipyard, sailed into Whitby harbour in 1954. Its crew had mutinied, taken over the vessel and had arrived on British soil seeking political asylum. No doubt the Stalinist regime under the Prime Minister Bolesław Bierut, which was then in power in Poland, kept this a secret.

The artefacts from the wreck of *General Carleton* kept on coming. There was a considerable variation in the manner of their preservation. For much of the starboard side of the ship the artefacts were encased in a sideritic concretion[3] which had to be removed by means of sheer hard work with a hammer and chisel. The port side was a different story: there the barrels of Swedish pine tar which comprised part of the cargo had been crushed and the tar had spilled out combining with the sand and sea-water to form a matrix which covered and preserved a number of artefacts. These survived in a mini environment protected by the ship's timbers and the cargo of iron bars. In bringing these items to the surface the divers became even more tar-covered that the sailors of old, and had to wear special suits to protect their equipment.

Many of these tar-soaked artefacts were remarkable not simply because they were preserved in such good condition but because they were preserved at all. Quantities of clothing and even fragments of paper survived. By the end of the season 538 items had been logged and taken back to the Maritime Museum at Gdańsk (*Centralne Muzeum Morskie*, or CMM) for the pains-taking and time-consuming work of their conservation and preservation by the dedicated team of conservators led by Beata Jakimowicz ably assisted by Wiesław Urbanski and Irena Rodzik.

Eventually a letter from Dr Ossowski reached the Literary and Philosophical Society of Whitby which is based in Pannet Park. The *Lit & Phil*, as it is commonly known, was founded in 1823[4], and maintains not only the museum, but also a large archive and library. Harold Brown, Honorary Archivist at the Lit & Phil, was asked to do some research on

---

[3] Analysed by Roman Chlebowski of the Univerity of Warsaw.
[4] One of the founding fathers of the Lit & Phil was George Young, author of *A History of Whitby* (1817).

9: The mouth of the river Piaśnica, showing the research vessel *Kaszubski Brzeg* anchored above the site of the wreck of *General Carleton*.

10: The *Kaszubski Brzeg* moored outside the Polish Maritime Museum at Gdańsk.

11: The bell of the ship *General Carleton*, the discovery of which enabled the wreck to be identified. This bell was rung every half hour when at sea.

12: The firehearth, which was among the earliest artefacts to be discovered, and the last to be raised. It was on this stove that the *General Carleton* cooks (William Parker, James Watson, Edward Walker, George Borne and James Woolf) would have made the hot meals for the crew.

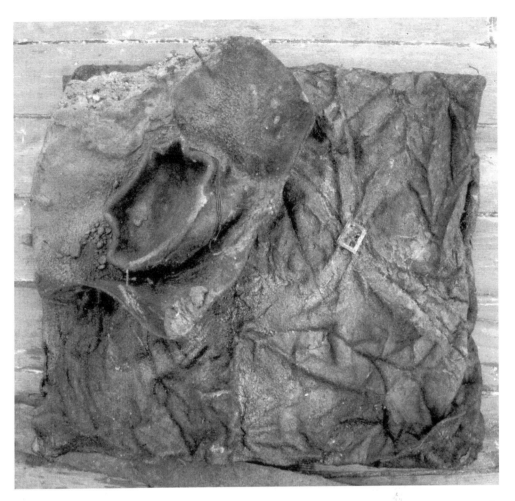

13: A hat and clothes as found in the wreck. The artefacts were covered in tar and sand, but in a remarkable state of preservation; it can be seen that these items were folded and put by their owner (probably one of the apprentices) carefully into his sea-chest.

14: Pieces of off-cut sail canvas have been stitched over a worn out felt hat, using sail twine, and the hat was then tarred. The resulting *tarpaulin*, the only one of its kind which has survived from the Eighteenth Century, would have been made by one of the crew of *General Carleton*.

15: A round brown wool-felt hat; a typical workman's hat of the period.

General Carleton. He had been engaged in sorting out a massive pile of dusty and disordered muster rolls which had been discovered in 1980 during refurbishments in the attic of the Whitby Seamen's Hospital in Church Street. These muster rolls were the original crew lists of Whitby-owned vessels starting in 1747 and continuing, in an increasingly attenuated form, for a period of more that 70 years. Their function was to record the payment of 6d per sailor per month at sea for a fund to provide for the *Relief and Support of Maimed and Disabled Seamen and the Widows and Children of such as shall be killed slain or Drowned in the Merchants Service* in accordance with an Act of Parliament of 1747. In Whitby the Seamen's Hospital, which had already been providing for such eventualities since its foundation in 1675, took over the organisation and implementation of this Act.

The Lit & Phil already had the official transcripts of these documents in a series of ledgers, but the newly-discovered original muster rolls often contained more accurate and more detailed information and were a valuable primary source. Harold had spent much time bringing order to these mouldering bundles of documents providing, for example, a complete set of muster rolls for the vessels in which James Cook served. Similarly he was able to find the muster rolls for *General Carleton* which covered all the nine years of the ship's existence. They were not only able to give the names of the main owners of the ship and of all those who sailed in her, but also to give the exact date when she sank. This information was sent to Dr Ossowski who was delighted and sent a return letter dated 6 February 1996 requesting more details about the crew, the ship, owners (Nathaniel and Margaret Campion) and especially the cargo it carried. This book is the product of the research which was instigated by this request.

The second season of excavation of the *General Carleton* wreck began on 10 June 1996 and, although hampered by a severe Baltic storm which halted work for over a week, produced a further 222 artefacts. It had been clear from the beginning that this was a very special wreck, and by the end of the second season it was evident that it was of massive importance. The items of clothing are of international significance, not just as rare examples of merchant seamen's clothing which have previously only been seen in illustration, but as examples of working dress from the period, from which so little survives. As Susan North, Head of the Textile & Fashion Department at the Victoria & Albert Museum in London has pointed out:

Prior to the 20th Century, clothing at all levels of society was recycled: passed on to family and servants, remade into children's clothing, sold to second-hand merchants...Even when extremely worn and no longer wearable, clothing was sold to the ragman, who recycled anything made of linen or cotton into paper...Wool was recycled into another fabric called 'shoddy' and after several more lives as garments, eventually shredded to stuff mattresses and all manner of upholstery.

Professor Lawrence Babits, Director of Maritime Studies at East Carolina University, made the importance of the *General Carleton* clothing artefacts quite clear, when he stated:

The clothing on the 'General Carleton' is the finest collection of well-dated 18th-century common male's clothing ever found.

But it is not just the clothing. There is a whole array of artefacts which together give us a clear idea of life aboard ship, and indeed ashore, in the 18th Century, which is why *General Carleton* has been dubbed *The Yorkshire 'Mary Rose'*. There are more details in the book *The General Carleton Shipwreck, 1785*, and the more significant items recovered are on permanent exhibition at the Polish Maritime Museum at Gdańsk, which is well worth a visit. There is talk of having an exhibition of some of the best of the *General Carleton* artefacts at the Pannett Park Museum, Whitby – and it would be wonderful for them to return for a while to the county in which so many of them were made over 230 years ago.

It was possible to do only a short period of work on the wreck in 1997 the highlight of which was the raising of the firehearth. Nothing was done in 1998. An attempt was made in 1999 to record the ship's structure in more detail, but the wreck had been totally submerged once more by the sand of the seafloor as a result of the stormy weather of the previous year, and work was abandoned. The ever-shifting sands of the seabed ensured that the wreck became visible once more in 2005, and although no additional work has been done on the wreck since 1999, there is still more that could be discovered and it is possible that in the future another team from the underwater archaeology department of the Polish Maritime Museum at Gdańsk will visit the waters off Dębki beach to learn more of *General Carleton's* secrets.

Chapter 3

1728 - 1762
Staithes and the James Cook Connection

The owner of *General Carleton* was Nathaniel Campion. The Campions were a family from the village of Staithes a few miles north of Whitby on the coast of what was then known as the *German Ocean*. Staithes was a lively place, more small town than village, making its living from the sea. Mainly this was from fishing – in the 18th Century a profitable business – and its harbour and Creekside were crammed with fishing vessels. Other sources of income were the nearby alum works at Boulby which required comparatively small vessels to fetch kelp, coal and urine and to export the finished product.

Many of the fishing and alum boats would have been built at Staithes, though the maximum size of vessel that could be built there was about 50 tons. Typical of the vessels built at Staithes was the 45-ton open boat *Midsummer* built in 1761.

We know of several vessels owned, and possibly built, at Staithes before 1762, such as *Amity* owned by William Frankland, *Mayflower* owned by Robert Truefitt (and lost 1749-50), *Blessing* and *Watson* owned by John Marshall and *Nelly* and *Nelly's Increase* owned by James Marshall.

Ships[5] were not officially registered until the Act of 1786, before that time we have to rely on other sources for information about ownership, mainly the muster rolls which usually give only one name as owner of a vessel. Small fishing vessels may have had only one owner, but larger ships were usually owned by a group of people, though there would be one organising owner, or *ship's husband*, who would be the name on the muster roll. Many people would have had part-ownership of vessels before 1786, of which we now have no record.

The Campions were also shipowners. Nathaniel's father Robert, who was a master mariner, owned the fishing boat *Mary and Jane*. His uncle Thomas Campion, a fisherman, married Elizabeth Jefferson who was the sister of John, owner of *Thomas and Richard,* and the daughter of Anthony Jefferson, who owned *Midsummer*, *Sally*, *Sarah* and *Triton*. The latter must have been of a considerable size, as it traded across the Atlantic to Carolina. Nathaniel's mother Jane was also a Jefferson[6].

Although it could not accommodate large ships, Staithes could still profit from them. In suitable weather large vessels might stand off and replenish stores and fresh water, which

---

[5] Vessels in the 18th Century were classified according to their rig. A ship was technically a three-masted vessel with each mast *square rigged* (ie with sails aligned across the ship). This distinguished a ship from other types of vessel. For example a bark (or barque) had three masts of which the front two masts (fore mast and main mast) were square rigged but the mizzen mast was fore-and-aft rigged (ie with sails aligned along the vessel). A brig had two masts, both square rigged; a brigantine had two masts of which only the fore mast was square rigged. However, as here, the word 'ship', then as now, was loosely used to describe any large sailing vessel, and I have taken the liberty of doing so regularly to avoid the endless repetition of the word 'vessel'.

[6] Probably the daughter of William Jefferson of Whitby. She had a brother Nathaniel whom, presumably, her son was named after. The Whitby Jeffersons may well have been distant cousins of the Jeffersons at Staithes and Newcastle .

would have been more convenient, and cheaper, than sailing into the crowded port of Whitby with the risks of delay and accidents caused by colliding with other ships.

A number of large trading vessels were owned or part-owned by inhabitants of Staithes, Staithes master mariners captained sizeable ships sailing out of Whitby, and Staithes seamen were among their crews.

Staithes was, and still is, difficult to reach overland. In the early 18th Century the road to Staithes would have been a muddy track difficult to travel on unless hardened by sun or frost. The main access to the town was by sea; but in spite of this there was also a great deal of overland travelling, mainly on horseback. The east coast was linked by networks of family and trade, and Staithes – though small – was part of this.

We get a good insight into this world through the diaries of Ralph Jackson who was at this time apprenticed to William Jefferson, hostman[7] of Newcastle. William Jefferson was the brother of John Jefferson of Staithes whose wife Eleanor née Allely was a cousin of Ralph Jackson the diarist. After his apprenticeship terminated, Ralph Jackson worked for his uncle Ralph Ward, who was a part-owner of the Boulby alum works, and also a diarist.

It was in this environment that Nathaniel Campion was born in 1728. Staithes is in the parish of Hinderwell, and it was there that he was baptized on 28 August. He was *born to the sea*, following in the family tradition, and was familiar with ships at an early age, being an apprenticed servant to a master mariner ship-owner probably at the age of 12 or shortly after. The Campions were connected with many of the established Staithes mariner families: in 1741 Nathaniel's older sister Mary had married John Galilee, and their children married into the Garbutt[8] and Weatherill families[9].

Nathaniel's uncle Thomas died in 1735. His widow Elizabeth was left with four children between the ages of eight and just under two. Within the year she had married John Saunderson at Hinderwell on 1 Aug 1736.

It was with William Saunderson, shopkeeper of Staithes, that James Cook was placed, at about the age of 17. This was arranged by Thomas Scottowe, who was James' father's employer at Great Ayton. He had noticed the young James, recognising in him signs of real ability which he nurtured by paying for his education at the local school. James' education there ended at the age of 13, after which he seems to have worked helping his father who was foreman of Airyholm, a farm owned by Scottowe. It was clear, however, as

---

[7] A hostman would provide colliers with coal, supervising the whole process from loading the coal to completing the paperwork. See *Bound for the Tyne* by Cliff Thornton, which contains extracts from Ralph Jackson's diary, with an explanatory introduction. Thornton has transcribed all Ralph Jackson's diaries which can be accessed on the Historic Cleveland website.

[8] Alternatively Garbut, Garbot or Garbort. There was no standardised spelling of surnames, and people would often spell their own names in a variety of ways.

[9] Hannah Galilee, the daughter of John & Mary, and niece of Nathaniel Campion, married William Weatherill in 1782. Her grandson George Weatherill (1810-1890) was the painter, known as *the Turner of the North*, many of whose pictures are on display in the Pannett Park Gallery at Whitby. George's son Richard was the author of the enormously informative book, *The Ancient Port of Whitby and Its Shipping*.

16: Staithes.

17: Boats at Staithes.

Young remarks, that James' *remarkable facility in the science of numbers* was *suited to some better employment*. Consequently Scottow arranged for Cook to go to Staithes as an assistant to William Saunderson, his wife's brother-in-law.

It has often been said that it was at Staithes, as he looked out from his room above the shop at the North Sea and the constant flow of vessels, that James began to dream of a life as a sailor. However, it seems likely that James had already decided that a life of adventure at sea was what he really desired long before he went to Staithes. Legend tells us that James as a young teenager loved to climb Roseberry Hill (or *Ounsbery*, as he would have known it), a local landmark from the summit of which on a clear day he could see the distant ships, sailing up and down the coast and dream of what they were carrying and where they were going, and what it would be like to travel in those majestic vessels, so much larger that the small house he was born in. Contemporary accounts suggest that Cook was determined to the point of stubbornness, and once the idea of a career at sea formed in his adolescent mind, he was firmly committed to ensure it happened. The small James would have told everyone, and that would include his father's boss, that one day he was going to be a sailor. In such a situation Scottowe's decision to arrange for him to work at William Saunderson's shop can be interpreted less as an attempt to ensure that a boy who was good at Arithmetic was given a chance to shine in the retail trade; but as an attempt to ensure that James was given the chance to be near the sea and to learn how to row and sail, and understand in a real way what the life of a sailor was like: to learn sea skills, and to test whether his dream of going for a sailor was a mere young lad's fantasy or a sensible commitment. In the process he would also have the chance to learn some life skills: more polish – the sort of manners and behaviour that are appropriate to a young man seeking to make his way in the world in a more busy and cosmopolitan environment than existed on the farm at Great Ayton.

But it was probably more than that. As Cliff Thornton has pointed out, William Saunderson was no small-time corner-shop owner; he was a wealthy man with a number of business interests who was well-known, well-respected and well-connected in the town. Thomas Scottowe knew this, and probably thought that if, after some time at Staithes, James Cook still wished to go to sea, then Saunderson could promote his career by using his connections among local master-mariners and shipowners, such as the Campions, the Jeffersons, the Marshalls, and the Wards. This would explain why Cook was not actually apprenticed to Saunderson, but was there on a kind of *ad hoc* basis; clearly he was not expected to stay in the shop-keeping business, and, indeed, he only lasted as a shopkeeper for about eighteen months, before taking a real apprenticeship with John Walker.

The Eighteenth Century was a time when who you know and who you are related to was important. Connections were everything when it came to securing contracts, finding jobs and, indeed, finding a wife. Family ties, which freely included third cousins, were important in business, and making the right marriage could extend your family to include some very valuable and influential new relations.

Adam Boulby has a fairly important role in this story. He was a master-mariner, shipowner and benefactor, living in Flowergate, Whitby. He was related to the Jeffersons and the Campions, his brother Thomas had married Jane Campion at Lythe in 1753. Adam's two daughters Dorothy and Esther ("Etty") were cousins of Ralph Jackson, and appear regularly in his journals. Adam's mother Esther (Hester) was a Chapman, a very well-established Whitby Quaker family; and numbered among her first cousins Solomon and Ingram Chapman (who both married daughters of William Linskill), and Abel who married Elizabeth the sister of John Walker. It is quite possible that Adam was instrumental in placing James Cook as an apprentice with the Quaker John Walker.

When he was at Staithes James Cook must have become acquainted with Nathaniel Campion, only two months his senior, who was already an apprentice at sea. Nathaniel's two elder brothers, Samuel and John, were even more experienced in the nautical life[10]. In 1747 Samuel was to be Mate of *Hopewell* and Master of her by 1750, and by 1751 John was Master of *Thomas & Richard*, owned by John Jefferson of Staithes, and Nathaniel was also a master mariner.

James Cook may well have been intrigued and excited by the tales of the sea the Campion brothers could tell him; Ralph Jackson records how the Jefferson household spent an evening rapt by John Campion's stories of his *Voyages* and *about the Custom's at Riga*. The life of the Campion brothers was exactly the career James Cook was wishing for himself, and he would no doubt take a keen interest in learning about the realities of the life on a Whitby collier in the North Sea trade.

It was in about 1746 that Cook abandoned his life as a shopkeeper and moved to Whitby to become bound apprentice for three years[11] to Mr John Walker Jnr. Interestingly the first ship that we know Cook sailed on was the *Freelove* in 1747, the master being another John Jefferson[12].

In 1748 Cook moved to another Walker-owned ship, the newly-built *Three Brothers*, which left Whitby on 14 June, with John Walker as master as far as London. Walker was simply trying out his new purchase, and intended John Jefferson to be master; however Jefferson was held up concluding the paperwork after his arrival at Whitby in *Freelove*, and had to catch up with *Three Brothers* as best he could. In the event she had already left London and Jefferson boarded her at sea; Robert Watson, a supernumerary mate who had been acting master for three days, being taken off the ship. On this voyage *Three Brothers* was sailing as a transport hired by the Navy Board. Several Whitby merchant ships had taken part in this nine-year War of the Austrian Succession as transports moving men and equipment. Weatherill lists sixteen such ships, besides *Three Brothers*, employed in 1748-9, including: *Hopewell*, Robert Eston[13], (owner Henry Cockerill), and *Olive Branch*, Thomas Holt master and owner. It is possible they were mainly engaged in bringing troops home, which was perhaps the only type of war work that the pacifist Quaker John Walker would permit his ship to be involved with.

The Treaty of Aix la Chapelle in October 1748 officially ended the war, and the Whitby transport ships returned to the coal trade once more. Cook continued in *Three Brothers*, travelling from Shields to London, bringing coals from Newcastle. In April 1749

---

[10] There was also an elder brother Robert, baptized in 1720; who died in 1763. Nathaniel also had a younger brother Isaac who was baptized in 1736; he also went to sea: his first voyage was as a carpenter on *Tryton* (owned by Anthony Jefferson) in 1757 when he was 20, by 1768 he was Master of *Dorothy and Catherine* (owned by Robert Galilee).

[11] Normally apprenticeship lasted 7 years, and boys started at about the age of 12-14. For older boys a shorter apprenticeship was available; James Cook was one of these, becoming what was known in Whitby as a *three years' servant*.

[12] Listed in the muster roll as being 32 years old from Sandsend; so possibly the John Jefferson baptised at Lythe 24 June 1713, son of John, or the one baptised also at Lythe 27 September 1719, son of Nicholas.

[13] Some ship names were very common, eg *Elizabeth*, *Good Intent*, *Endeavour*, *Sally* and (in ports such as Whitby with a large number of Quaker shipowners) *Friendship*. The usual way of distinguishing a vessel therefore was to give the name of the master immediately after that of the vessel, as here. I shall use this custom throughout.

he finished his apprenticeship, after which he continued in *Three Brothers* as a seaman, apart from an eight-month season on *Mary* in 1750, and then in 1752 he became Mate on *Friendship*. It is more than likely that James Cook kept up his acquaintance with the Campions, as they certainly would have come across each other in Whitby, Shields or London by accident if not by design.

When James Cook was an apprentice, or *servant*, he lived with the Walker household in Haggisgate (not – as is commonly supposed – in Grape Lane. The building there, which now houses the excellent Cook Museum, belonged to John Walker's parents, and he only moved into that house in 1752 when James Cook was no longer his *servant*). Once Cook's apprenticeship was over he became a seaman, and as such had to find his own accommodation. When a ship had reached port and the sailors were no longer needed they were discharged, and they had to find their own way home. This happened to James Cook. In 1750 he was on *Mary*[14], and discharged in London on 5 October. He needed to get back to the North East where he lodged, and from where *Three Brothers* would sail at the beginning of the following season.

What happened next has always been something of a mystery: the muster roll for *Three Brothers* for 1751 lists a Robert Storpe, seaman, and mentions his previous voyage. Unfortunately, it is not clear what is written, but it appears to be: *The Hopewell Sam. Ca:Campling*. Although this is somewhat cryptic, it seems clear that Robert Storpe was on a ship called *Hopewell* of which Sam Campling was Captain in 1750, and it gives the nature of the voyage by adding 'Do' to a list of similar dittos under the phrase *To London*. Immediately under Robert Storpe's name is that of James Cook, which has a ditto under *The Hopewell Sam. Ca:Campling* but not in the *To London* column, suggesting he sailed on the same vessel, but not when it went on a trip to London. The only *Hopewell* with a master whose name is anything like 'Sam Campling' is the one captained by Samuel Campion; indeed *Camplin* is regularly used as an alternative for *Campion* in the Hinderwell parish records[15]. The muster roll for this vessel for 1750 exists, and there is no mention of James Cook, so naturally it has been assumed that he was not on this vessel. The *Hopewell* muster roll shows a crew of 11 starting at London on 13 June for what is clearly a series of coal journeys between Shields and London. The original carpenter Robert Taylor, of Whitby, was discharged (perhaps for injury or illness) at Shields and was replaced on 9 November by Thomas Barrick. Oddly they took on at the same time an additional sailor from Newcastle called Robert Stanhope. Why would a crew, already up to strength, all of whom (apart from the mate) were from Whitby and who have worked together for at least four and a half months, suddenly decide to take on a new sailor from Newcastle? A possible answer is that Robert Stanhope is none other than James Cook's friend Robert Storpe (whose name is spelled Storupe in the *Three Brothers* muster roll for the latter part of 1751), and that Samuel Campion had given free passage from London to Shields to his old friend James Cook, and included the latter's comrade Robert as an added bonus. As they were working their passage and therefore not being paid, there was no reason to put their names on the muster roll for this journey. At Shields Cook disembarked, but Robert Stanhope presumably

---

[14] Also a seaman on this voyage with James Cook was Charles Noddings, who was similarly discharged at London on 5 October. Charles Noddings later became a master mariner and owner of the 230-ton Selby-built ship *Providence*. He was the uncle of John Noddings who sailed as servant on *General Carleton*.

[15] For example, Nathaniel's brother John is referred to as *John Camplin of Staithes* in the baptism entry for his son Nathaniel in April 1749, and *John Campion of Staithes* for that of his son Samuel in January 1750.

needed the money and was allowed to sign on for the last 26 days of the ship's voyaging, and for that time is entered on the muster roll. The following year they were shipmates on *Three Brothers* until they were discharged together on October 28.

Cook sailed on *Three Brothers* in 1751, with Robert Watson (the supernumerary mate on her maiden voyage) as captain. Ralph Jackson records that after having a business dinner on 27 February 1753 on board *Hopewell* with Samuel Campion, he went with John Campion and *Watson, Master of one of Walkers ships of Whitby* (ie *Three Brothers*) to go on board the *Peggy Man of War*; but by then Cook had left *Three Brothers* to be Mate on *Friendship*. Ralph also mentions *Freelove*, another of Cook's former vessels, later in the same year (9th and 10th July) when Nathaniel Jatkin, master, and John Walker himself arranged with William Jefferson that he should load *Freelove* with Tanfield coals.

Ralph Jackson the diarist knew the Campions well: Samuel, John and Nathaniel were all masters of ships on the coal trade. This would involve sailing to Shields where they would moor their ship. There they would hire a horse and ride to Newcastle, or sometimes William Jefferson, having received news of the arrival of their ship, would send Ralph down to greet them and invite them to stay at his house until the ship was cleared[16]. There are frequent references to one or other of the brothers dining or staying overnight at William Jefferson's house. These occasions often included a visit to Mrs Hudspeth, who lived in Newcastle. Mrs Hudspeth was Anne (née Jefferson): sister of William, wife of Robert Hudspeth and mother of William (Billy) who was a great friend of Ralph's – their both being of an age. The reason why the Campions made these visits is presumably their family connections, either through their mother Jane or their aunt Elizabeth (both née Jefferson).

Ralph clearly was particularly fond of John Campion whom he refers to both as *Mr John Campion* (as befits the respect shown to a master mariner and customer, who was more than 10 years his senior) and *Jacky* (as befits a close friend and companion). They were already friends by the time Ralph started his diary in October 1749, as one of the first entries is *John Campion and myself took a walk*. John Campion was present when Ralph Jackson was *bound* (apprentice), as was *Cousin Jefferson*. John and Ralph went hunting together, and Ralph was invited on board *Thomas and Richard*, of which John was the master, to dine or drink tea. Nathaniel was somewhat nearer Ralph's age and they did more juvenile activities together such as going round Newcastle *to the Glass house* where they *saw a Soldier whipt*. This in November 1751 when Nathaniel was 23 and Ralph was 15.

It was about this time that Samuel Campion moved to Whitby, and in 1752 he married Jane, the daughter of the late Joseph Holt, and brother to John Holt, master mariner and part-owner of the Dock Company, and also to Thomas Holt, owner of *Olive Branch*. Two months after his marriage, Samuel brought his new wife up to Newcastle, where she stayed with Mrs Hudspeth. On the same visit Samuel and Ralph went shopping for shoes.

Ralph Jackson gave up writing his diary in September 1753, but started it again only to tell of the sad story of the death of John Campion:

Wednesday May the Twenty Ninth 1754. My Master came from the Exchange and brought News that Mr. Jn° Campion of Staithes Master of the Thomas & Richard was lost in Bullrow at Riga in going from one ship to another…
and that later the body of *M' Jn° Campion was hall'd up by an arm by some sailors that were weighing their anchor in order to come from Riga about a week after M' Campion was so unfortunately drowned.*

---

[16] Granted permission to sail by customs and the city authorities.

He then writes nothing more in his diary until March 1756. This single entry in what would otherwise be a lacuna of two and a half years is an eloquent testimony to his fondness for his friend Jacky.

On the death of his brother John, Nathaniel became master of *Thomas and Richard*. In 1756 Ralph Jackson spent the night on board this ship, on which he had passed merry times with John, but this time as guest of Nathaniel.

1756 saw the beginning of the Seven Years War, which has also been called both the first World War, and another spasm of conflict in the second Hundred Years War against the French. For many Whitby ship owners this was a further opportunity to help the war effort and to make good money by hiring out their vessels as transport ships. For James Cook it was an opportunity to expand his horizons as a sailor. He enlisted in the navy, *having a mind to try his fortune that way.*

Most of the Whitby ships continued in their usual trade. *Jenny*, Robert Boulby; *John*, John Jefferson (owned by Moorsom & Holt); *Richard and Thomas*, Richard Knaggs; *Lyde*, Thomas Ward (owned by Thomas Lotherington); *Olive Branch*, Matthew West; *Royal Briton*, John Holt master and owner; and *Tryton*, Samuel Campion (owned by Anthony Jefferson) were all making coal journeys between Shields and London during the war, to *keep the home fires burning.*

Elizabeth, Thomas Simpson (owned by Benjamin Ward); *Hero*, George Burton of Staithes; *Prince of Wales*, George Potts; *John and Elizabeth*, James Linton (owned by Thomas Holt), and *Lyon*, Henry Fowler (owned by Adam Boulby) were among the Whitby ships that were transports. Sailing into a war zone was dangerous, and there were casualties. Five men died on *Lyon* in 1757, two of them at Charlestown, and a further two the following year. The average age of these seven seamen was 21. The vessels *John and Elizabeth* and *Lyon* were also casualties of the war.

It must not be forgotten, though, that life in home waters was also dangerous. Crossing the North Sea could be perilous; *Hope*, master and owner Benjamin Lotherington, was lost in 1756, probably on a voyage to Norway for timber, and *Leviathan*, Yeoman, also of Whitby, was lost in the North Sea the following year. The coasting trade had its own risks: Captain Henry Taylor of North Shields, who served his apprenticeship on a Whitby collier in the 1750s, wrote: *There are few coasts as dangerous as the east coast of Britain. Sandbanks lie a considerable distance from, and out of sight of land; from the Spurn to the Thames the channel is between sandbanks and the main land, and frequently between one bank and another.* In 1757 *Benjamin* of Whitby was stranded on just such a sandbank off Winterton on the Norfolk coast, and *Friendship* of Whitby was among a number of vessels which foundered off the Suffolk coast in a storm.

Accidents at sea could have tragic consequences. Whaling ships were required to carry a surgeon, but ordinary merchant ships did not. There would be a medicine chest aboard, and well-preserved glass pharmaceutical bottles from just such a chest were found in the *General Carleton* wreck. If a mariner was injured at sea he would be lucky if the Master or perhaps another member of the crew had some basic first aid skills.

Figs 2a & 2b: *Medicine bottles recovered from the wreck of General Carleton*

John Holmes, servant on board *Harwood*,[17] Joseph Gibson, in 1758 *had the misfurton* [misfortune] *of Jamming his finger very much the 6 april.* This was just two days after they had left Shields. The muster roll laconically reports the sequel: *& Continued until he died.* His death, *at Sea*, was on 10 July, over three months later; we can only imagine the pain he experienced from the moment of the accident through all that time as the wound suppurated, became infected and then fatally gangrenous. Although the vessel must have been in port several times over those long weeks there is no record of his being sent ashore to see a surgeon, and one can only assume that any treatment he received was at best amateurish and ignorant, with bandages that would not be very clean.

On 28 April 1756 George Raine, eldest child of George and Isabel, started on his first voyage at sea as a *servant* on the Whitby collier *Elizabeth*, Thomas Ward (owned by Miles Breckon and Thomas Holt). There were three other servants making their maiden voyage on the vessel, so they probably gave each other moral support, comradeship and encouragement. On 17 August, after less than four months at sea, George had an accident: he fell down into the hold while *Elizabeth* was at Shields loading coal, and was badly hurt. The muster roll records that he languished eight days and then died; the expenses incurred for the surgeon and for George's lodging and *Funril* [funeral] are carefully noted as totalling £2-2-2 (£313; £3,400)[18]. He was twelve years old. His brother Isaac, not yet one year old at the time of George's death, was later to sail on *General Carleton*.

After the burial of George Raine, *Elizabeth* loaded her cargo of coal and sailed for London but off the coast of Suffolk she came to grief on the sandbanks at Orford Ness and was totally wrecked; fortunately the crew seem all to have survived. Another servant on *Elizabeth* who was experiencing his first taste of life at sea was Peter Booth. He continued

---

[17] William Frankland, whose son Simeon was to sail on *General Carleton*, was on this voyage. *Harwood*, with Henry Thompson as master, had been a privateer in 1747 with one of her 16-man crew, William Clark, a designated *Gunner*.

[18] For the monetary system and equivalent modern values see Appendix One.

his apprenticeship the following year, aged 15, on *Olive Branch*, where misfortune dogged him again: after less than 5 months aboard he was *Sick* and *Sent ashor* at Shields on 4 July, 10 days later he was back on *Olive Branch* only to be discharged sick once more this time at London on 2 August. He was not back as a member of the crew until 22 November when he was picked up at London for the run home to Whitby. He concluded his apprenticeship on *Speedwell*, becoming a seaman in 1763. William Smith of Danby, another novice servant who was on *Elizabeth* when she sank, sailed on *John and Elizabeth* first in 1758 when she was a collier, and again the following year when she was a transport ship when she was lost, probably in Canada, on 23 October 1759. William apparently survived the trauma of his second shipwreck in little over three years, but there is no record of what happened to him thenafter.

Chapter 4

September 1763 - 1777
Building Ships

1763 saw peace once more. Nathaniel moved to Whitby which offered more prospects of wealth and advancement. In this he followed the career pattern of his brother Samuel.

By this time Samuel owned two ships, *Triton*[19] and *Diamond*. *Triton* was owned by Anthony Jefferson in 1747 but Samuel Campion, who had probably owned a part-share before, had become the main owner by 1756 when it was employed in the coal trade, with Richard Knaggs as master.

Nathaniel had also followed his brother into the ship-owning business and had become owner of *Thomas and Richard*;[20] Edward Theaker of Staithes later stated that he had gone to sea at the age of ten [in about 1764] and had been *Apprentice of Seven Years in the Ship Thomas & Richard belonging to Mr Nathaniel Campion of Whitby.*[21] Nathaniel had been a part-owner before that time, and he could have been influential in transferring *Thomas and Richard* from the coal trade to the Baltic trade. Certainly as early as 1752 the ship was regularly sailing to Riga, which it continued to do after the outbreak of war. In 1761, after returning from Riga, she set out again, still with Nathaniel Campion as master, as a transport for Guadaloupe, with several other vessels under the protection of *Augusta*. This is the latest record of Nathaniel being an active master mariner, and when he returned he probably gave up sailing, to concentrate on being a ship-owner. To add to his portfolio, he decided to commission the building of a new ship. This was *Valiant*, which was built in Whitby in 1763.

Nathaniel followed his older brother's example not only by marrying, but by marrying into the same family. On 6 June 1762 he married Margaret, the daughter of John Holt. His brother Samuel Campion had married Jane, the sister of the same John Holt.[22] John was a master mariner, the eldest son of the late Joseph Holt, one of the founders of the Dock Company. John, with his brother Thomas, owned a quarter share of the Dock Company, as tenants in common. Although only a second-generation Whitby resident, John Holt was already prosperous and well-connected with others in the same line of business – as the Campions were in Staithes; it was a mutually advantageous match. Such things were important as at that time there was no clear distinction between business and family connections.

---

[19] Ralph Jackson at some stage had a part-ownership of *Tryton* and of *Thomas and Richard*.

[20] John Jefferson of Staithes had died in August 1759. He left Samuel Campion his 1/16th part of *Triton*, his part (possibly ½) of *Thomas and Richard* to Nathaniel Campion, his part in *Midsummer* to his brother Anthony, and bequests to Adam, Dorothy and Esther Boulby. The bearers at his funeral included Mr Pease, Mr Sanderson, John Holt and William Skinner.

[21] In his Trinity House petition dated May 1816. Edward Theaker had married Mary Burkinell, daughter of John, ship-owner. He became a master mariner but had become *unfit for any sort of Employment* being at times *quite deranged*. Edward received 6/- per month from Trinity House to support himself, his wife and his two young daughters Dianah and Indiana.

[22] Which must have made it rather confusing for the children of Nathaniel and Margaret, as their uncle Samuel was also their great-uncle.

There is a matching pair of miniature portraits of John Holt and his wife Martha, née Storm, in the possession of the Whitby Lit & Phil, which have been dated by Susan North to the 1770s. John is wearing a brown coat with a slight collar, and has lace cuffs, both of which would have been fashionable at the time, though his wig would have been a bit *passé*.

Fig 3: John Holt, based on the miniature in the Whitby Lit & Phil.

His pose is one that was deemed appropriate, and is recommended in the eighteenth-century manual of polite style *The Rudiments of Good Behaviour* which comments that: *the Bend of the Elbow, at its due Distance, will permit the right Hand to place itself in the Waistcoat easy and genteel.* He would have been in his mid to late 50's, the image of a visibly prosperous member of the Whitby shipowners.

The author Daniel Defoe wrote briefly about Whitby in his *A Tour Through the Whole Island of Great Britain*, published in 1725. He notoriously disparaged the Esk as *a little nameless river, scarce indeed worth a name*; but what he meant was that the Esk was navigable only a small way upstream (to Ruswarp Mill) and therefore Whitby did not have a large import and export trade serving a vast inland area as Hull did. However, he did add

35

that Whitby had *an excellent harbour, where they build very good ships, and many of them too, which makes the town rich.* He was right in that the harbour is what made the town prosperous. Gaskin pointed out that *no more convenient site* for shipbuilding could be found anywhere than *the inner harbour of Whitby, sheltered as it is from every storm, with a depth of water sufficient for that time.* Lionel Charlton, whose *History of Whitby* was published in 1779, claimed that the harbour could accommodate over 250 ships, and certainly it was one of the few havens along the dangerous north-east coast where collier ships, plying their valuable trade between Newcastle and London, could shelter from fierce storms, and could overwinter. For this reason it was a valuable asset, and various Acts of Parliament were passed to raise money for the improvement of the piers and harbour. Young, writing some 40 years after Charlton, stated that it was in about 1730, when *the harbour became so improved as to accommodate large vessels*, that shipbuilding really became a major industry in Whitby, expanding from the already impressive position that Defoe had mentioned.

Although there was a major boom in ship-building in Whitby, it is quite difficult to be exact about the details of the industry, and to know with any certainty, with a few notable exceptions, who built which ship before the early 19th Century when the names of shipbuilders appear regularly in the Whitby ship registers.

Because there was no mass of exports and imports through Whitby with the consequent wharves and warehouses taking space on the riverbanks, the Esk was lined with shipbuilding sites instead. The noise and bustling activity must have been impressive, and perhaps oppressive too as Charlton recorded that building work started at 5.00am.

Defoe had commented that England was *a trading, improving nation* in which *fortunes of families taking different turns, new trades are every day erected, new projects enterprised, new designs laid.* This was certainly true of Whitby, with regard to shipbuilding, and allied trades.

On the east bank of the Esk a large piece of river frontage *near unto a place ... called Spittle Bridge* was owned by the Dock Company, which had been founded in the 1730s by four enterprising master mariners, Joseph Holt, William Barker, John Reynolds & John Watson (whose share was soon owned by John Kildill), to build dry docks for repairing ships. A double dry dock was finished in 1734, and a single one followed shortly after, which was advertised as being where *Ships may be repair'd at very reasonable Rates.* Lionel Charlton added that the work was done *very completely*; but he was probably exaggerating (and not for the first time) when he added the claim that the costs of repairs at Whitby were cheaper *than in any other part of Great Britain*, though they were certainly competitive. When *Hopewell*, Samuel Campion, *Came in to repare* in April 1751 and *Hannah*, Thomas Galilee, spent time in April 1758 *Reparin in ye Dock* at Whitby it was most likely to these dry docks that they came. The work was not only reasonably priced, but speedily executed as there were *plenty of Carpenters* – as Henry Hugill pointed out to the Navy Board in 1781 when he asked to have his transport ship *Archer* repaired at Whitby rather than at Deptford.

Lionel Charlton was absolutely right when he stated that the building of the dry docks was good for the trade of Whitby as *many strangers* [ie non-local residents] *are also thereby induced to come into our port for the sake of repairs.* As wooden ships needed constant

18: The Inner Harbour at Whitby. On the opposite (east) bank, right, is the site of William Coulson's shipyard, later occupied by Ingram Eskdale. Beyond that, north of the waterside shed and the barely visible mouth of Spital Beck, lies the site of the Dock Company shipyards and dry docks.

19: Whitby Parish Church on East Cliff. The row of white houses beneath the church are on Henrietta Street (Haggerlyth) which John Wesley was so scathing about. Henrietta Street used to be much longer, but much of it was destroyed in 1787 when part of the cliff fell into the sea.

20: The graveyard of Whitby Parish Church. Many are buried here who have no memorial; and many are mentioned on these headstones who are not buried here, but who died or drowned in far-off places.

21: Runswick Bay. It was here that Thomas Cassildine, of the 1st Regiment of Dragoons, was murdered in 1776 while attempting to seize contraband goods from smugglers.

maintenance, this was a lucrative business; Charlton estimated that between £10,000 and £12,000 a year was annually paid for repairs done in the dry docks (some £11-14 million in today's money). They were especially profitable in winter as vessels were laid up for at least a couple of months (usually between mid December and mid February) when the North Sea was at its fiercest and insurance was at its most expensive – if it was obtainable at all. The docks, in addition to its permanent workforce, also provided seasonal winter work for ship's carpenters to cope with the increased demand at that time.

The rest of the Dock Company's site comprised two shipyards which were let out at various times to various people for various enterprises. The Dock Company also owned ships, so it would be likely that they also built most of the ships they owned. Certainly part-owners of the Dock Company, and members of their families appear regularly as shipowners. For example *Fly* is recorded in the muster rolls as being owned by the Dock Company between 1757 and 1768, but after that time by James Reynolds and Co; similarly *Good Agreement* is listed as being owned by the Dock Company between 1762 and 1768, but in 1772 is owned by John Holt. James Reynolds and John Holt are respectively the sons of John Reynolds and Joseph Holt, founders of the Dock Company.

Because the Dock Company's shipyards were let, they allowed for a number of rather temporary shipbuilding concerns: members of the Reynolds, Holt, Barker and Richardson families seem to have set up partnerships in a dizzying array of combinations: Reynolds and Co, Holt & Reynolds, Holt and Barker, Holts & Richardson and finally Holt and Richardson.[23] Business in Georgian times was often a family affair, and companies formed and dissolved almost casually.

The lease of a yard from the Dock Company also seems to have acted as a start for shipbuilders who later moved to a yard of their own: William Coulson started on Dock Company land before occupying the Whitehall shipyard on the other side of Spital Bridge, and Benjamin Coates leased a part of the Dock Company property before moving across the river after his father died. William Simpson leased Dock Company land before branching out and building himself a dry dock further along the shore. Unfortunately it could not be kept dry and was filled in; and it was left to his son Richard to successfully build a dry dock in about 1760, reusing material from his father's failed attempt, on the other side of the river on land allegedly recovered from the sea (roughly on the site of the present station). This site was later used for the shipyard of the Langbornes, and it is highly probable that when George Langborne built the 251-ton *Henrietta* for Nicholas Piper in 1764 it was in a leased yard on the Dock Company premises.

The west bank was the site of the shipyard of Jarvis Coates who built the *William and Jane*, the earliest Whitby ship for which we know the shipbuilder[24]. His eldest son, also Jarvis, built a yard at Boghall to the south of his father's yard; and after the father's death the younger son, Benjamin, took over the Bagdale Beck end of things. Jarvis junior went bankrupt in 1743[25], after which Benjamin seems to have taken over his brother's yard. On

---

[23] See Appendix Two for further information on the bewilderingly complex intermarriage between the Whitby ship-building families.

[24] *William & Jane* survived long enough to appear in ship registration, at which time it was said to have been built in 1717. Jarvis (or Gervase) Coates died in 1738, aged 78. There were earlier shipbuilders: the parish registers mention of a Matthew Shipton, master-builder [ie master ship-builder], who was buried in 1723.

[25] The first reference in the London Gazette is for 24 Sept 1743, and was still not completed by 27 August 1754, by which time the Assignees of the bankrupt's estate, Richard Ellison and Henry Walker had both died.

Benjamin's death in 1757, Thomas Fishburn bought the shipyard formerly owned by Jarvis, and Robert Barry took over Benjamin Coates' former yard, and shortly after, in about 1763, that was subdivided, Henry Barrick taking a part on the south end and Thomas Hutchinson the northern end moving his shipbuilding works from what is now the site of Angel Inn yard.

So, when Nathaniel Campion wanted someone to build him a ship in 1763, there was no shortage of shipyards. *Valiant* was to be a large ship: a 1773 list of Whitby ships gives her measured tonnage as 360, and she was accurately measured by the Navy Board in 1780 as 341.44 tons.[26] Of all the available shipbuilders in Whitby at that time, Thomas Fishburn was the one who seems to have specialised in larger vessels, so the likelihood is that he built *Valiant*.

It was in Thomas Fishburn's yard, in the following year, that the 370-ton *Earl of Pembroke* was built for the master mariner Thomas Millner; she was later bought by the Navy, renamed the bark *Endeavour* and became James Cook's vessel during his First Voyage. It is likely that *Valiant* looked rather like *Endeavour*, only slightly smaller, though she was probably ship-rigged.

Of course it is a possibility that, as Nathaniel was about to marry into the Holts, he had the ship built by the Dock Company, or a family firm that operated from Dock Company premises. If this were the case, it may well have helped ensure a positive and enthusiastic response when Nathaniel was asking John Holt for his daughter's hand in marriage.

The naming of a ship was only finally decided when the ship was launched, and it is possible that the name 'Valiant' referred in some way to the Seven Years' War which was being fought at the time, maybe to the recent dramatic capture of the port of Havana from the Spanish after a costly two-month siege which ended on 14 August. It was at the engagement at Havana that Adam Boulby and Benjamin Ward, both probably relatives of Nathaniel Campion, lost ships that were acting as transports. If *Valiant* was named to commemorate this event, then she would have been launched after the news of the victory reached home and possibly before the massively unpopular Treaty of Paris, signed on 10 February 1763, which ended the war and which involved the return of Havana to the Spanish. Certainly we know that *Valiant* was in London on 18 May with coal from Newcastle, with Nathaniel as master; it seems he came out of retirement for a season to test out his new acquisition, after which he employed William Herbert as captain. William Herbert was born at Goathland in 1728 and sailed on *Mary* in 1747 and again in 1750 when one of his fellow seamen was James Cook. He was master of *Isabella* (a ship owned by James Atty senior and named for his wife) when she was lost on 7 October 1756 – apparently with no loss of life.

Nathaniel and Margaret's first child, Jane, was born 13 May 1763 though not baptized until 30 November of that year. She was presumably named for the recently-deceased Jane Campion, Margaret's aunt and the wife of Nathaniel's brother Samuel. Samuel was to marry another Jane in September 1763 – Jane Brewster. Unfortunately Nathaniel and Margaret's daughter Jane died when she was three years old. Their next child, Martha, also died young. By the beginning of 1777 Margaret had given birth to seven children, of whom three were already dead.

---

[26] The formula for measuring the tonnage of ships gave a fractional tonnage in 94ths. *Valiant* was 341 $^{44}/_{94}$ I have taken the liberty representing 94ths as decimal 100th parts. For more information on ship tonnage see Appendix One.

Though their family life was fraught with tragedy, Nathaniel and Margaret prospered in other ways. They were living in Baxtergate virtually next door to the house (now the George Hotel) of Margaret's brother John Holt and his wife Mary. The Poor Rate Assessment Book shows that John Holt was assessed for a 6d rate, but that Nathaniel paid a shilling – twice as much – which would suggest that he was seriously wealthy and able to live in some style.

James Cook returned to Whitby at the very end of 1771 after his first voyage on *Endeavour* for what was intended to be a private visit to see his former master John Walker and some of his friends, but which turned out to be something of a triumphal entry into town, greeted by a delegation of leading citizens, and accompanied by an enthusiastic mob of fans to Grape Lane, the home of John Walker. His stay was brief, but it is very probably that he would have made a point of seeing Samuel and Nathaniel Campion, his friends for many decades who had encouraged him when he was a teenager at Staithes.

Although these were years of peace, life was not untroubled for the inhabitants of Whitby, as in the country as a whole. For many life was hard, and often short. Young points out that several inhabitants of Whitby lived to an impressive old age, which was fine if you were well off. But in the yards of Whitby, some of the tenements on Boulby Bank, and the seaward end of Haggerlyth (Henrietta Street), which John Wesley described as the *very sink* of the town *where people of any fashion were ashamed to be seen*, families were squeezed together by poverty in filth and squalor, untouched by education, and without even basic sanitation. Here life was cheap and disease was rife, and the sons would enlist in the navy and army not through patriotism or a desire for adventure but simply because they would be clothed and regularly fed.

It was not just the poor who suffered from disease. The inhabitants of Whitby were crammed largely into a very small area, and in a time when medical knowledge was still fairly basic an outbreak of disease could spread very quickly among rich and poor alike. In 1772 there was a serious epidemic of smallpox in Whitby, starting in the summer and continuing into early 1773. Although anyone could catch smallpox, the young were most susceptible as many of the adults had survived the disease in earlier life and had immunity. In 1771 there were 126 burials in the Parish Church with less than a quarter of them being children under 5 years old; in 1772 this had leapt to a frightening 290 burials with children under five accounting for well over half of them. With fatality among the under fives increasing almost sixfold, hardly a family would have been untouched by the tragedy.

One of the early victims was the 7-week-old baby George, son of the shipbuilder Nathaniel Langborne and his wife Ann. On 6 September there were six burials, including Martha[27] the young wife of George Atty, their son having been baptized only six weeks earlier. Thomas and Dorothy Heavisides buried their 10-year-old son John on 9 September, their 2-year-old son George on the 22nd and their 4-month-old daughter Eleanor on 1 October – the same day on which Mary Storm and her husband Matthew, master-mariner and cousin to Margaret Campion, buried their 4-year-old daughter Elizabeth. Thomas and Ann Smales buried their children Thomas (8), John (5) and Elizabeth (1) all within 15 days in October. Henry Richardson and his wife Hannah lost their eight-month old daughter Hannah on 11 November and their three-year-old son Isaac a fortnight later; Henry's sister Mary and her husband George Galilee's two-year old Isabella died three weeks after Isaac.

---

[27] Martha née Coates, daughter of William. George was the son of James and Isabel Atty; in 1782 George married Susanna daughter of William Barker.

On the 9 November there were nine burials of whom eight were children whose average age was less than three. George Langborne, brother and shipbuilding partner of Nathaniel, and his wife Mary buried their five-year old son John on 15 November.

The epidemic continued into 1773, but was abating. Elizabeth, the 8-year-old daughter of Henry and Elizabeth Boynton, was buried on 4 February; Henry had been master of *Thomas and Richard*. One of the latest victims was the 9-day-old Katherine, daughter of Jonathan Lacy ropemaker of Spital Bridge, who was buried on 21 March 1773 in the Quaker burial ground. The baby would have been the first cousin of Mary who later married William Holt, Margaret Campion's brother[28].

In 1775 we find Nathaniel Campion as one of the Whitby Seaman's Fund Trustees, a prestigious appointment, putting his signature to a letter to the Collectors of Customs at Newcastle, Sunderland, Hull and Whitby itself to protest that they are clearing vessels to leave port without checking to see if they are up-to-date with their muster roll payments, and requesting that they do not give ships clearance to leave until such debts are paid. According to the Fund's letter-book only Newcastle replied, and their response was that they would send a list of the vessels not paying, which was not the hoped-for response.

Thomas and Richard and *Valiant* were both proving to be successful, and neither seems to have had trouble paying the muster roll money on time. In 1767 *Thomas and Richard*, master Henry Boynton, was sailing between London and Memel (present Klaipėda). *Valiant*, after a couple of years as a collier, traded mainly from London and Newcastle to Norway, Memel and Riga. In 1767 we know that she made two voyages to Norway followed by two voyages to Riga, returning each time to London. She was probably importing timber, hemp and tar – all vital products for making and repairing sailing ships. At that time she had a crew of 14 men and boys. One of the boys was probably William Thorp, apprentice to Nathaniel Campion, who drowned at Whitby, aged 18, in February of the following year. It is likely this was from an accident during the busy preparation of *Valiant* for the new year's sailing season.

Although these were some of the all-too-infrequent years of peace in the 18th Century, and ships therefore did not need to travel in convoy, it was good practice – provided it was possible without causing unnecessary delays – to sail with another friendly ship. When Whitby ships arrived in port they were often accompanied by other Whitby ships: when *Valiant* reached Gravesend from Memel in June 1770 she sailed in with *Mackerel*, William Hustler[29]; and when she was at the Port of London from Memel in November 1772, so was *Pallas*, Thomas Holt[30].

In 1773 there was a change of master for *Valiant*; William Herbert was replaced by Thomas Pyman. William Herbert went to be master of the 187-ton *James and William* built for George Atty, and launched at Whitby on 23 March 1773.

Thomas Pyman was the son of a master mariner, also called Thomas, and Elizabeth née Sneaton. The elder Thomas had moved to Whitby from Sandsend, a small coastal village between Whitby and Staithes, lured by the prospects and opportunities that Whitby

---

[28] It is only in the Quaker burial records that the cause of death is given. Some of the deaths mentioned here may not have been part of the smallpox epidemic.
[29] William Hustler (1738-1801) was son of Thomas and Ann née Smales. He was master of *Mackarel* (1767-1780), and possibly shipbuilder after that. He married Ann Skinner whose brother William married Elizabeth Holt, Margaret Campion's aunt. He was not the same person as the William Hustler who was master of *General Carleton*, but was probably his cousin.
[30] Margaret Campion's brother.

offered, and marrying a local Whitby girl. He clearly made a success of his career, as he was living in Flowergate in 1737 and paying a penny poor rate, and five years later, living in the Old Market Place he was assessed for twice the amount of poor rate payment, suggesting an impressive increase of his fortunes. In 1747, when the Whitby muster rolls begin, Thomas the elder was master of *Robert*, a collier with a crew of fourteen, so a vessel of comparable size to *Valiant*, and it is presumably as master of *Robert* that he appears in Ralph Jackson's diary for May and June of 1753. In October of that year he was master of *Jane*. The owner, John Stonehouse, had started out as master at the beginning of the year, but drowned at Bremen on 1 June; his brother Robert then took over as master, but lasted only three months – probably due to illness. Thomas Pyman the elder was clearly a man trusted to do the job well in a situation where the crew, no doubt superstitious as were most sailors, may well have regarded the ship as cursed.

His son Thomas was baptized at Whitby parish church on 4 January 1736 (new style)[31], the fourth son. The children were *bred to the sea*, Thomas' elder brother William and his two younger brothers Henry and John all became master mariners. The young Thomas was apprenticed to Adam Boulby, probably when he was 14. This would mean he was a *servant*, and would sail on Boulby ships in the season, and live in the Boulby household during the winter, learning the art of navigation and the various skills requisite to being a master mariner. It is clear that for many apprentices their master became over time a close friend, as the young James Cook did with John Walker; and something like this seems to have been the case with Adam Boulby and Thomas Pyman. Adam had lost three daughters and his only son Robert in infancy by the end of 1746, and to some extent Thomas might have fulfilled the role of substitute son for him.

Once Thomas completed his apprenticeship, he was appointed mate (in 1758), and shortly after as master, of John Mellar's collier *Whitby*. On the strength of his promotion, increased pay and status Thomas married Esther Williamson on 9 December 1759 by licence in Whitby Parish Church; the witnesses were Elizabeth Williamson and John Pyman.

By 1768 Thomas Pyman was back with Adam Boulby as master of his ship *Dorothy and Esther*. The collier was originally named for Adam's two daughters, but since then, as we learn from the diary of Ralph Jackson, Esther – Ralph's little cousin Etty – had died in London of a fit, at the age of fourteen. It is often commonly assumed that in the days when infant and child mortality were common, parents took the early deaths of their children more calmly; but there is wealth of evidence to show that this was not the case, with fathers as devastated by their loss as mothers. Shortly before Etty's death her sister Dorothy, only 17, had married Dr Henry Askew of Newcastle.

Thomas would have known both Dorothy and Esther as little girls from his time as a servant in Adam Boulby's house and would be have been happy to sail a ship named after them. The fact that his wife's name was also Esther would have been an added delight. When Thomas Pyman was master, *Dorothy and Esther* mainly journeyed between Newcastle and Norway or the Baltic.

---

[31] Technically Thomas' baptism was in 1735 as before 1752, in the old style calendar, the year began on 25 March, so January 1735 would be the month after December 1735. This was usually written 1735-6, as people were confused by this even in those days. I have retrospectively used the new style dating, as I have throughout, and called it 1736.

**Fig 4: Martha Holt, née Storm, wife of John, mother
of Margaret Campion and mother-in-law to Robert Boulby**

There is no doubt that Thomas Pyman was an excellent master mariner, and clearly loved his work. Young records that he was *45 years a captain* in which time *he was never shipwrecked, nor stranded, nor captured; nay, he did not even lose an anchor or a cable* and − even more remarkably − *he was never intoxicated.* This was a master mariner worth employing, and it seems likely that, in 1773, when Adam Boulby was 70, he was prepared to let Thomas Pyman go to be master of *Valiant*. Again there is a family connection: Adam's nephew Robert, the oldest surviving male member of the younger generation of Boulbys, was married to Martha Holt, the younger sister of Nathaniel Campion's wife Margaret. Robert Boulby also commissioned the building of a ship called *Margaret and Martha*, possibly named for his sister-in-law Margaret Campion and his wife Martha. His mother-in-law was also called Martha, a member of the multitudinous Storm family from Robin Hood's Bay.

It is not clear when the troubles in America turned into war. It is generally considered that the War of American Independence (or the Revolutionary War as it is known in the

46

USA) began with the skirmish at Lexington, on 18 April 1775, but in fact both sides had been sliding into this conflict for some time, mainly due to intransigence on the British side – in spite of a considerable body of opinion on both sides of the Atlantic that were against the idea of a war. Bickham rightly summed up the mood of the country when he wrote that *the British went to war with great reluctance.* The official proclamation of war was not made until August of 1775, and the American Declaration of Independence, which marked the change of status from colonies in revolt to a nation fighting for its political autonomy, was 4 July 1776. The British, however were moving troops into the area in 1774 which in itself is not a sign of imminent war. At a time when there was no police force, difficult issues of law and order were dealt with by sending in the military. In 1776 soldiers of the 1st Regiment of Dragoons were sent to Staithes to attempt to control the endemic smuggling on the north Yorkshire coast. This was not an easy task; Thomas Cassildine, a member of the regiment, was *cruelly murdered at Runswick in attempting to seize some smuggled goods.* He was buried at Hinderwell on 18 June.

However the size of the troop movements in 1774 was of sufficient magnitude to suggest an imminent conflict, and in part may have provoked it. At first the Government believed that what they were dealing with was a revolt and not a revolution: a bunch of disaffected radicals based on Boston. The early British strategy was to focus attention on Boston and, by subduing that city, end the troubles. Consequently the Government sent large numbers of troops to Boston from 1774, to reinforce the British position there. The lesson of the previous wars had been learnt by the shipowners of Whitby: hiring out vessels to the Navy Board could be a profitable business even though one might have to wait some time to receive the money, and compensation was payable if the vessel was lost while in government service. Not surprisingly Whitby transports were among those that sailed in 1774 from Cork to Boston: *Dorothy and Catherine*, Robert Galilee[32], sailed with *Drafts & Recruits for Gen Gages Army* leaving on 8 April, taking some 71 days; *Hunter*, W Hunter, and *Lively*, J Grey, both sailed on 7 May arriving in fewer than 60 days, the former with 125 soldiers of the 38th Regiment of Foot and the latter with 94 men of the same regiment and two of the 65th. *Pallas*, Thomas Holt[33], carrying soldiers of the 64th Regiment, sailed from Spithead on 16 April, reaching Boston in 57 days. Nathaniel Campion's *Thomas and Richard*, Cuthbert Park, was also a part of this operation, leaving Portsmouth on 19 April with 138 men of the 43rd Regiment of Foot aboard and sailing to Boston, stopping at Quebec *en route* to pick up a number of artillery men. The following year *Thomas and Richard* made a trip to Halifax to ferry 79 soldiers of the 65th Regiment from there to Boston, arriving on 8 May in time for the Battle of Bunker Hill.

The idea that occupying Boston in force would soon end the revolt was a serious misreading of the situation, and although the British won the battle of Bunker Hill in June 1775 it was a Pyrrhic victory. The British decided to evacuate Boston, which eventually happened in March 1776 but would have occurred earlier if there had been sufficient transport ships available.

By late 1775 it had become evident that it was not going to be quite so easy to suppress the American *rebels* as had at first been believed, and when word reached Britain that the Americans were threatening Canada, so recently and so dearly won from the French,

---

[32] Robert Galilee was Nathaniel Campion's nephew: the son of John Galilee of Lythe and Nathaniel's elder sister Mary. He would be 23 when he sailed on this voyage.

[33] This was Margaret Campion's younger brother. When he set out on this voyage he was 23 and had been married just over a year to Esther née Stockton.

it was clear there would not only be serious fighting, but that it would have to be on several fronts. The government in London believed that the most seditious states were those in the north and that is where the first serious offensive was targeted. A prodigious reinforcement of troops and equipment was to be sent to North America in the hope of making a decisive difference and of bringing the conflict to a swift end.

What ensued was a massive logistical exercise; some 10,000 troops had to be gathered from all parts of Britain, and from the garrison in the Mediterranean, together with auxiliary troops from our allied German states Brunswick and Hesse-Cassel which contributed 4,300 and 12,000 troops respectively. The Navy Board, which was in charge of transports, was given the colossal task of providing the shipping and provisions to transport these troops together with their equipment, ammunition, horses (and a number of wives) to North America. Syrett adds that: *No military operation of this size and scope had ever before been attempted.* The demand for transports was similarly unprecedented, and Whitby ships, mainly crewed with Yorkshire sailors, rose to the challenge; the owners no doubt tempted by the fact that the Navy Board had raised the payment for transports from the pre-war level of 9s a ton per month to 11s.

Vessels submitted for service as transports were inspected at one of HM Dockyards. Samuel Campion's *Apollo* was surveyed at Deptford on 26 December 1775 and was measured as 361.56 tons, described as being eight months old, with her *Bottom Single*[34] and, together with the Whitby ship *Harmony* which was assessed at the same time, was described as being *roomly and having good Accommodations fit to serve as Transports for Foreign Service*. A great deal can be learnt from these surveys; for example, *Success Increase* was lying at Church Hole, but was inspected in Fletcher's Way on 25 August 1775. She was a Whitby-built 321.18-ton brig, three years old, measuring 66ft 10ins by 22ft 2½ins, and her body form was described as *full*. Her lower deck had been laid, her gratings had been made and she had cabins for three officers and 166 men; she would be ready to enter into pay on 28 August.

A certain amount of shuffling around of the troops in the Mediterranean was needed to free up the best fighting men for America. On 24 November 1775 *Garland*, Levi Preston, and *Success Increase*, J Jackson, left Gibraltar taking respectively new recruits and members of the 51st Regiment to Port Mahon, thence they sailed with soldiers from the 1st Regiment of Foot to Portsmouth; *Archer*, William Coats, left Gibraltar with members of the 1st Regiment for Portsmouth two days after *Henry*, J Taylor, sailed with soldiers of the 13th Regiment for the same destination.

Peace and Plenty, Elisha Preston, (28th Regiment) and *Rachel and Mary*, Rowbotham, (33rd Regiment) were both involved in the disastrous North Carolina expedition which aimed at supporting the Loyalists there; but due to incompetence and adverse weather conditions the transports did not arrive at Cape Fear until May, four months after the North Carolina Loyalists had proclaimed their allegiance in expectation of immediate British support and had been soundly defeated by the American forces. *Peace and Plenty* then took her complement of soldiers to Long Island.

Love and Unity, Andrew Easterby; *Three Sisters*, Thomas Readshaw; *Argo*, George Tate; *Saville*, William Hustler[35] and *Royal George*, Joshua Kneeshaw, all sailed from Cork to Boston, leaving in April and May and arriving in June and July, with members of the 44th

---

[34] Hulls were sheathed (sometimes with copper) or doubled, given an extra wooden outer layer to protect the ship from damage caused by collision or being eaten by the 'ship-worm' *teredo navalis*.
[35] This was the William Hustler who was later to be master of *General Carleton*.

and 45th Regiments. These were part of the main offensive which resulted in considerable success – most notably in the capture of New York by General Howe: a popular victory which gave rise to celebrationary verses of dubious quality, such as this which appeared in the *London Advertiser* on Monday 19 August 1776:

> *Why, Lord Howe is landed*
> *And not a boat stranded.*
> *So soon as he could spy land,*
> *On Staten's small island,*
> *With bomb boats and yatches,*
> *(As say the dispatches)*
> *Safe and sound, and as snug*
> *As a bug in a rug.*

New York remained in British hands for the duration of the conflict, and served as the main base for many of the military operations of the war. The war seemed to be going well: also in 1776 the British captured and occupied Charlestown.

Several Whitby ships were involved in another of the major cross-Atlantic convoys of troops in 1776: the carrying of the troops from Brunswick and Hesse-Cassel to Canada. The Whitby vessels employed were: *Apollo*, John Adamson (owner Samuel Campion); *Elizabeth*, Joseph Holt (Thomas Holt); *James and John*, George Watson (James Atty); *Martha*, William Holt (master and owner); *Pallas*, George Bell (Thomas Holt); *Prince of Wales*, George Pressick, (John Holt); *Providence*, James Watson (John Chapman), and *Royal Briton*, William Sleightholm (John Holt). It is likely that *Harmony*, John Staincliff (John Addison); *Laurel*, Henry Boynton (William Barker), and *Minerva*, Matthew Robinson, also sailed in this convoy. The large number of Whitby vessels involved reveals the importance of the town in providing transports for the Navy Board.[36] Interestingly we have an account of life on board one of these Whitby transports on this very voyage. It was written by Lieutenant Du Roi the Elder, an officer in the 680-strong regiment of Prince Friedrich Durchl, part of the Brunswick contingent seconded to the British army. Du Roi travelled on *Prince of Wales*; which carried 213 men (though he does mention the presence of some women as well). Lieutenant Haynes, the agent for the fleet, was on board *Pallas*, and the 32 horses of the staff officers and adjutants were on *Martha*, which Du Roi describes as *one of the best and newest ships not so liable to roll*, explaining that such a ship *in the nautical language of the English* was called *"a good seaboat"*. The modifications for accommodating the horses were that their deck was covered in coarse sand, and their stables were narrow and padded; additionally there were broad straps which were put under the horses to support them when the sea was rough (and there was plenty of that).

After taking an oath of allegiance to the King of England, the German troops were embarked over a number of days. They anchored at Cuxhaven on the 22 March 1776 before venturing out to sea. Du Roi remarks on the cleanliness of the ship and the efficiency with which *every morning the whole ship is washed with sea-water*; this was no doubt very

---

[36] Several other Whitby vessels were employed as transports in 1776 which are not mentioned in this chapter. These included, *James and William*, William Herbert, previously master of *Valiant*, (George Atty); *Liberty*, Zachariah Garbutt, (G Chapman); *Lyde*, Robert Hodgson, (Thomas Lotherington); *Margaret and Martha*, William Preston, (Robert Boulby); *Myrtle*, William Walker, (Joseph Barker); *Speedwell*, John Steward, (Thomas Holt); *Spring*, William Dunn, the brother of Robert Dunn who sailed on *General Carleton*, (William Barker); and *Venus*, Richard Thursby, (Matthew Storm).

necessary as he also mentions the widespread incidence of sea-sickness at the beginning of the voyage in open sea, and whenever the waves were high.

He also has praise for the captain, George Pressick, whom he described as *a man of honourable, upright character, full of life,* cheerful, knowledgeable, well-read, *without the coarse character common to other seamen,* and possessing all the good *qualities of his nation,* and who – by his behaviour to his passengers – won the friendship of the officers and the respect of the men.

On 28 March they were at Spithead, and George Pressick took Du Roi on a tour of Portsmouth. It was while they were there that they learned that they were going to Canada, more specifically to Quebec which was being besieged by the Americans. They were also joined by nine more transports which carried British artillery needed for the re-capture of Quebec if the city had already fallen by the time the reinforcements arrived

On 4 April the signal to sail was given, anchors were weighed, and the convoy fleet of 36 vessels moved out in two lines led by the frigate *Juno,* with the frigate *Blonde* (with General Burgoyne on board) at the back to guard the rear and to hurry up the slower ships. Du Roi proudly asserted that it *made a fine spectacle.* On 8 April they passed Land's End and were in the open Atlantic. There was more sea-sickness; but the majestic convoy, guided by *Juno* by means of an elaborate system of pre-arranged signals both visual and audible, made good speed, mainly covering more than a hundred miles a day, averaging over 4 knots[37].

On 16-17 April there was a storm from which they emerged unscathed apart from the fact that George Pressick lost his hat and *speaking tube* (megaphone), and the cook lost his favourite dog. They were less fortunate with another, and fiercer, storm which blew up on the night of 23 April when the ship sprung a leak; but as there was so much water in the ship, despite the crew who had been busy at the three pumps for ten hours, the location of the leak could not be found. The captain feared that unless the storm abated there was real danger that the ship would not reach Newfoundland. The next morning the soldiers helped with the pumping, and William Pinkney the carpenter eventually found the damage and made a temporary repair, but it was impossible to mend it properly while the sea was so rough. Unfortunately on the following day the wind was even more violent, and the pumping continued; a sail was shredded in the gale, and the wheel broke – which was repaired by the long-suffering William Pinkney. On the 26th the wind abated somewhat and the leak was stopped entirely and once the remaining water was pumped out all was calmer; but the fleet had been separated in the storm, and it took all of the next day to reassemble the scattered ships. Then it was business as usual, the convoy covering 124 miles on the 28th, and no doubt George Pressick was at last able to take a well-earned rest.

The number of birds that were seen announced that they were near land. It also became much colder and on the 29th a fire was lit in the great cabin. On 2 May the occasional mist turned into thick fog: it became impossible to see where any of the other ships were so one of the ship's guns was fired every quarter of an hour, and there had to be a drummer on deck all night to signal the vessel's location and thereby avoid collisions. *Juno*

---

[37] To gauge the speed of a ship a triangular piece of wood (the *log*) was thrown overboard. It was attached to a line into which knotted cords had been interwoven at 42 ft intervals. The number of knots on the rope that had been paid out in 30 seconds (measured by a sandglass) gave the speed of the ship in knots. See Appendix One.

was also firing cannons to guide the convoy in accordance with the pre-arranged signalling code.

Fortunately the fog lifted at about midday the next day, and the lead revealed a depth of 32 fathoms. A great joy was that they were able to fish[38], and caught fresh cod to eat, which was cooked with mustard and butter. They had been surviving on meagre and unpleasant food as their original supplies had been eaten, rotted or gone mouldy, and the drinking water was foul and smelt so vile that they had to hold their noses to drink it.

They were now in danger from American privateers, and the frigates were put in a state of preparation for action. The transports posted an additional watchman with a loaded gun to keep a look-out during daylight. The *Prince of Wales'* six 6-pounder cannons were kept loaded, and orders were given for what to do if attacked. Those on board were tense and nervous, most of them were young, far from home and with no idea of what dangers might lie ahead. It had been a month since they left Portsmouth, and the news that was then available about the progress of the war was already several weeks out of date: anything could have happened in the interim.

They passed Cape Breton Island on the 13th, on the 17th adverse winds meant they spent endless time near Ile d'Anticosti tacking and making very little headway. To add to their troubles it snowed heavily the following day, the snow on deck freezing overnight. When they had set out from Brunswick and at Portsmouth there had been blissful sunny Spring weather, near the Azores the temperature had soared and now it had plummeted below zero. On the 20th the convoy entered the St Lawrence. Although very few in the fleet had been here before, some of the ships had done so as transports in the previous war; certainly *Prince of Wales*, with George Potts as master, had been part of the fleet of 119 transports that sailed with a British force of 9,200 men under Major General James Wolfe which had captured Quebec from the French in 1759. On that occasion James Cook, sailing master on the 64-gun *HMS Pembroke*, had carefully charted the river so that the following fleet could avoid becoming grounded or wrecked. This time the shipmasters had Cook's charts to hand.

On the 25 May the fleet anchored between the Island of Bic and Cape St Benabé. The frigate *Surprise* was there having come downstream to meet them. Two officers came on board *Prince of Wales* and told them that the siege of Quebec had been lifted and the Americans had been driven out of Canada. The 50-gun warship *HMS Isis* with three frigates (including *Surprise*), three victuallers and transports carrying the 29th Regiment had pushed through the ice to relieve the Governor-General of Canada and Commander of the army, Sir Guy Carleton. Carleton had attacked the besiegers with 800 men destroying their batteries, capturing ordnance, taking 300 prisoners, and ending the siege. This news must have been a great relief to the weary troops.

On 1 June they finally reached Quebec, but the Brunswick soldiers who were ordered to stay for a while in Quebec had to remain on their ships, while repairs on their barracks were completed. They finally disembarked on 14 June after 90 days on board.

At home the Navy Board realised it still did not have enough transports, and in June 1776 raised the rate to 12s 6d per ton per month. This was very persuasive, and it was no doubt this that prompted Nathaniel Campion's joint decision to hire *Valiant* out to the

---

[38] Catching fish was a valuable addition to a sailor's diet, in addition to being a pleasant pastime. A hank of fishing rope with a hook at one end was among the artefacts excavated from the *General Carleton* wreck.

Government and to commission the building of a new ship. He knew that he wanted Thomas Pyman to be master of the new vessel, so he ordered him to hand over command of *Valiant* to Richard Thompson, the mate, when the ship next came to port, and to make his way, all expenses paid, back to Whitby. Consequently Thomas Pyman left *Valiant* at London on 5 July 1776. The next day she sailed, with Richard Thompson as master and William Hebron as mate, to Cork. Cork was one of the main victualling centres for the British fleet so it was possible that *Valiant* became a victualler rather than a transport. Certainly between 6 July 1776 and January 1779 she sailed regularly between Cork and London.

A new vessel was timely. The Navy Board's strategy had worked and by the middle of 1776 they had over 400 ships in the transport service, which had a dramatic effect of the nation's shipping, one official remarking that the Navy Board had left the country drained of ships. Trade still had to continue, and the Navy needed to build, equip and repair its own vessels which required a large amount of timber, canvas, iron, tar and ropes. There were valuable contracts to be made for selling and transporting these goods.

Nathaniel Campion had a master for his new vessel, now he needed someone to build it. Ship-building in Whitby had been continuing to flourish even before the war; and since Nathaniel Campion commissioned *Valiant* there had been many changes: there were more shipbuilders, more ships, and more ships being built for shipowners outside Whitby. Price and quality were certainly important factors in ensuring that by the late 18th Century Whitby had established itself as a premier ship-building port. Charlton claimed that, at the time he was writing (c1778) there were *generally twelve or thirteen large ships on the stocks*, of which about half were built for Whitby inhabitants, and the total sum of new ships was 24-25 a year.

Nathaniel had a larger choice of shipbuilders. Thomas Fishburn, Henry Barrick, Thomas Hutchinson and Robert Barry were all in business still. There were ships being built in the Dock Company shipyards, one of which was probably occupied by the firm of Holt and Barker, which comprised John Holt, Margaret's brother, and Joseph Barker, who are mentioned as shipbuilders in Bailey's Directory for 1781 and were already in business by 1779 as they were importing timber from Danzig on *Traveller*, Robert Anderson, in November of that year.

Richard Simpson's dry dock was occupied by William Hustler[39] *for some time* then sold to the Langborne brothers, Young suggests around 1777. However George and Nathaniel Langborne had been building ships since at least 1764 when they built *Henrietta*, and ten years later they built the 295-ton *Diligence* (later Captain Cook's *Discovery*). It is likely, therefore, that the Langbornes started their shipbuilding career, as so many others seem to have done, by leasing one of the shipyards from the Dock Company, before accruing sufficient capital to buy the yard on the opposite side of the river from William Hustler. It is likely that the shipbuilder Hustler was the same man who was master of *Mackerel* between 1767 and 1780; if this is the case then he is unlikely to have begun his shipbuilding enterprise until 1781.

There are a number of other candidates who are possibilities, but who are not mentioned by George Young, or for whom we have evidence of their activity a few years later and who could have been building ships in 1776-7, these would include Ingram Eskdale and Abel Chapman. Perhaps the most intriguing of these other possibilities is that

---

[39] Not the same William Hustler who was master of *General Carleton*; but probably a cousin.

General Carleton was built by John Shepherd, and that Nathaniel afterwards recommended him to his brother Samuel. This is conjecture. As reported in the *London Gazette*, John Shepherd was declared a bankrupt in 1777, leaving a *Ship upon the Stock, partly built by the Bankrupt*. Samuel Campion had filed a suit, so presumably the half-built ship was his, and he had already paid a deposit.

It is tempting to assume that family connections might have led Nathaniel Campion to choose Holt and Barker, as John Holt[40] was his brother-in-law. Certainly it is important to remember that at this time that business and family decisions and finances were inextricably intertwined.

If Charlton's figures are correct then it took about six months to build an average-sized ship. With demand for ships high, and with at least a dozen ships being built in Whitby at any one time, there was probably a fairly long waiting list. It is possible that Nathaniel Campion used his family connections not so much to put work the way of a relative, but to jump the queue of owners wishing to commission ships.

Compulsory registration of shipping did not come in until 1786, a year after *General Carleton* sank, so we do not know the exact official measurements of the ship, though the deck measurements were taken at Stockholm in August 1785: 105ft 3ins (32.08m) long and 29ft 9ins (9.06m) across. In 1782 she was surveyed for the Victualling Board and was measured as being 380 tons. She was likely to be ship-rigged.

Nor do we know who owned her. It is very unlikely that *General Carleton* or *Thomas and Richard* or *Valiant* had only one owner. Nathaniel Campion was clearly the commissioning and managing owner but it was very unusual for a large vessel to be owned by one person. The advantages of multiple ownership were that the risk was shared and that it was possible for a range of people to invest in shipping without the headache of commissioning and managing a ship. The only person in the 1787 Whitby ship registers who is the sole owner of a sizeable ship is James Atty, sailmaker, who owned the 195-ton Swedish-built vessel *Charlette*; but then he could afford to be the only owner of this one ship, as he was a part-owner of twenty-one others at Whitby, besides four more which were registered at Newcastle.

We do know that at some time Nathaniel Campion was a part-owner of *Martha*, *Wisk* and *Peggy* because these ships survived to appear in the ship registers, which list their owners. Although Nathaniel Campion was dead by 1787, these three ships list *the executors of Nathaniel Campion* as being part owners. *Martha*[41] (326.72 tons, main owner William Holt) had eleven owners, *Wisk*[42] (272 tons, main owner John Holt) and *Peggy* (393 tons, main owner Nathaniel Campion) both had six. It would seem likely, therefore, that *Valiant* and *General Carleton* would have had at least five other part-owners besides Nathaniel. It is very probable that three of them were Samuel Campion, John Holt and Thomas Holt – all of whom appear as owners of *Peggy*, and in at least one other of the three ships. I suggest that Thomas Pyman would also have owned a, perhaps comparatively small, part of the new

---

[40] This John Holt was married to Mary Millner, daughter of Thomas Millner, master mariner, and shipowner. It was Thomas Millner who was the master and owner of *The Earl of Pembroke*, later Cook's *Endeavour*, which he had built for him by Thomas Fishburn in 1764.

[41] William Holt was master of *Martha* (1774-8), followed by Isaac Chapman until at least 1793.

[42] John Holt was master of *Wisk* in 1777, followed by Widget Stonehouse (1777-82) and then by Matthias Sidgeworth until at least 1787.

ship. It meant that he would always have a job and could take on servants, and it meant that Nathaniel Campion was sure of retaining an excellent master mariner for his new vessel.

News of the war trickled back from across the Atlantic, both reported in the press and told by the crews of the returning Whitby transports: William Holt on *Martha* had arrived back in London on 8 November; John Adamson on *Apollo* on 6 December, and William Sleightholm on *Royal Briton* on Christmas day. When Nathaniel Campion heard about how Guy Carleton had lifted the siege of Quebec and driven the American army from Canada, he decided to call his fine new ship *General Carleton*, honouring him as a British hero in a war that was rather short of them. When the military authorities heard of what had happened they were at first pleased, and Carleton had been made a Knight of the Bath; but Burgoyne, eager to advance his own career and rather piqued to be second in command, had returned to London where he had been spreading the word that Carleton had been weak and had failed in his duty when he had not followed up his advantage by pursuing the rebels and inflicting a decisive defeat on the enemy. The result was that both King and Government turned against Carleton who, although he remained as Governor of Canada, was stripped of his command of the army in Canada – a position that was given to Burgoyne.

This incident illustrates one of the reasons why the war in America was lost: many of the generals were rivals, using influence with the powers that be to further their own careers. The Government responded by appointing a number of men to different commands, moving and replacing them on a regular basis, without always making it clear what their authority was and who was to outrank whom in combined operations. There was never one general in total command of the British forces.

Fighting a war from an office in London is not the same as being in the field; Carleton was a realistic general and knew that if he stretched his lines of communication too far and too thin in difficult terrain he would make himself vulnerable – as Burgoyne was to discover for himself when, in a similar position, he was surrounded and forced to surrender with 5,700 men at Saratoga on 17 October 1777.

If Nathaniel Campion knew that Carleton was facing critical opposition at home then the naming of the ship could also have been a politically-charged vote of support. In which case, when he heard of the events at Saratoga, his feelings of incredulity and misery at such a catastrophic defeat may have been tempered with just a small degree of smugness that Burgoyne got his come-uppance.

Chapter 5

1777
General Carleton **Leaves Whitby**

General Carleton was probably launched in the latter part of January[43]. The launching of a new ship was always something of an occasion. A time of anxiety and expectation for the builders and owners; but a free show for the inhabitants of Whitby, as those that were not at work crowded in and round the shipyard to get a good view, or possibly on the opposite bank where they may observe the spectacle more clearly with less pushing and jostling – and possibly with less chance of having their pocket picked.

If she was built at Fishburn's Yard, as seems most likely, then the scene can be imagined. Thomas Fishburn emerging early from his fine new house above the Yard, with his brother John, to supervise the arrangements and to ensure no tragic accidents occurred. It was important that the ship moved easily down the slipway, which involved a great deal of soap, tallow, and hogs lard, at the same time ensuring she did not take the water too quickly, or roll over on her side. Thomas Fishburn had some of his strongest and most experienced men to knock out the chocks and to control the movement of the ship with ropes, wedges and launching spikes.

Nathaniel would be among the onlookers with his wife Margaret; coming from a nautical family she viewed the proceedings with an experienced eye, she had almost certainly joined her husband on some of his voyages on *Thomas and Richard*. The other part-owners would be there: Thomas Pyman, Nathaniel's brother Samuel, and Margaret's brothers John and Thomas. Samuel would be accompanied by his second wife Jane and his son John who, aged 22, was master of his father's recently-built ship *Apollo*, which had been launched in 1774, the same year as William Holt's ship *Martha*. John Holt, who also owned a share of *Apollo* and *Martha*, would probably be with his wife Mary and her father Thomas Millner – not only to see *General Carleton* being launched but to see how the building of the ship *Wisk* was progressing, due to be launched later in the year, of which John was the main owner and Thomas Millner one of the part-owners.

Suddenly there was an excited murmur, growing louder and then sinking to almost silence as *General Carleton* began to move down the slipway. It was a tense time. There was much fevered activity among the launchers, and some shouted commands; but the ship took the water easily. The tide had been well-judged, and she floated well and upright. There was a sudden release of tension as the crowd burst into cries of "Huzza! Huzza!"

The onlookers drifted away, leaving those more immediately involved to look forward to the launching supper. When *Henrietta* was launched in 1764 the launching supper was provided by *Strong*, presumably Ralph Strong the innkeeper, at a cost of £3-9-8½ (Over £4,000).

However, when a ship was launched she was little more than a basic hull, with the decks, and lower parts of the mast. We do not have the accounts of a ship built at Whitby in 1777, but the accounts of the Whitby ships *Three Sisters* (1761), *Henrietta* (1764, by George Langborne) and *Ann* (1787, by Thomas Fishburn) survive. The cost of the hull in these three

---

[43] This is based on the gap between the launching of a ship and its first voyage, where both dates are known. It seems to be about six weeks.

cases varied from £4-8s per ton (*Three Sisters*) to £4-12s per ton (*Henrietta*), so it would be sensible to suggest that the cost of the hull of *General Carleton* would be within this range and to estimate it at £4-10s per ton which would give a figure of £1,710. The total *cost to sea* of these vessels ranged from 1.7 to 2.2 times the cost of the hull, so *General Carleton's* cost to sea can be estimated as around £3,350 (£3,840,000).

Much had still to be done. Post-launching expenses would involve such items as, buying and fixing the rigging and sails, glazing the cabin windows, buying a suite of anchors and a stove (these last two together costing £80 in 1761 for *Three Sisters*), buying at least one ship's boat and to a whole range of internal fittings by ironmonger and carpenter. After that there would be a vast amount of different consumables to be purchased and loaded. This would of course provide valuable employment for local businesses[44] and craftsmen, though it is impossible to pick out names with any degree of certainty. However a list of people and their occupations compiled from the Whitby parish records (the PR list) can help identify some possible candidates while in no way claiming to be conclusive. For example, contemporary glaziers who could have worked on *General Carleton* were John Rigg (who also appears as a plumber and glazier in Bailey's 1781 Directory), Walter Wilson, John Renton, Stephen Dickinson and William Dickinson; this last was paid £10 for his bill as *plummer & Glazier* in the fitting out of *Henrietta*. There are 41 blacksmiths so there is not much help here – any of them could have worked on the structure of *General Carleton* or have made the firehearth; Roger Rickaby was paid £197-7-7 (£250,000) for his work as blacksmith for getting *Henrietta* ready for sea. Anchors and the ship's bell are more specialised areas, but could have been within the scope of some blacksmiths. The PR list does not mention any such specialists though John Brignall, *blacksmith* in this list, appears as an *anchorsmith* in Bailey's 1781 directory, so in the absence of better information he can be considered a likely contender for providing *General Carleton's* suite of anchors. There are six boat-builders in the PR list: Thomas Atkinson, Thomas Duck, Henry Harland, Robert Marshall, Henry Rowland and Thomas Storry (these last two also appear in Bailey's 1781 Directory). In 1764 Thomas Duck supplied *Henrietta* with a *Long Boat &c* for £18-15-9 (£24,000), and A *New Boate* was bought for *Three Sisters* in 1777 for nine guineas (£11,000), but the builder is not named.

The most expensive of the post-launching expenses were for sails and rope. Sailcloth making in Whitby was a major industry by 1777 though, as Young informs us, a fairly recent one, starting when Jonathan Sanders set up a manufactory in 1756 – before which time sail canvas used in Whitby had to be imported. Sanders' business flourished and two years later Christopher Pressick began a sailcloth business at Ruswarp, moving first to Boulby Bank and in 1777 it moved to Elbow Yard[45]. Shortly after Pressick started his enterprise, Christopher Ware set up a similar business at Bagdale, convenient for the shipyards on the West Bank, and in 1767 John and William Chapman started their sailcloth business at Spital Bridge, convenient for the Dock Company yards.

---

[44] Rosalin Barker, in her fascinating article *Tea for the Cabin, Milk for the Boys and Butter for the Ship*, estimates that the value of victualling and chandlery purchased in north-eastern ports by Whitby-owned ships was in the order of £50,700 pa (the equivalent of an amazing £63 million today).
[45] There is a document in the North Yorkshire Deeds Registry which suggests that Nathaniel Campion, Thomas Holt and Christopher Richardson took over this sailcloth manufactory on the death of Christopher Pressick, who was buried at Whitby on 11 July 1782. I am indebted to Dave King for bringing this to my attention.

These manufactories were not like the massive centralised mills of the later industrial revolution, though they were very busy and conditions cannot have been easy or pleasant. The Sanders business was actually carried on at three separate locations, one of which was at Guisborough, each with about a dozen looms, though all the looms of the Chapman works do seem to have been in one building. Flax-dressing and bleaching was also carried out at these manufactories, as well as weaving. The swiftly mushrooming business of sailcloth manufacture not only supplied the increasing number of vessels being built in Whitby itself, but also had a flourishing export business. On 7 October 1777 Jonathan Saunders agreed a contract to deliver to the Navy Board at Deptford, within 12 weeks, 160 bolts of canvas of varying grades from 16 bolts of number 1 grade (the coarsest) to 8 bolts of no 8; the largest amount was of 60 bolts for the comparatively finely woven no 6 grade. A bolt was slightly longer than 38 yards. Saunders completed the order on 16 January, but was four bolts short, which were delivered on 13 March. He received £450-11s (£500,000). The firm of John and William Chapman had a similar order on the same day. On 8 December 1777 Jonathan Saunders and Christopher Pressick both agree to identical contracts for 200 bolts to be delivered at Dartford within 12 weeks.

Clearly the sailcloth weaving industry of Whitby in just 21 years had grown into a major commercial enterprise. The PR list mentioned above contains only one person, Thomas Fernie, described as a *sailcloth maker*, but there are 7 individual bleachers, 63 flaxdressers (including three called *heckler*[46]) and 127 weavers, most of whom would probably have been weaving flax for canvas sails, though flax would have also been woven for making duck for sailors' trousers, other workmen's clothes, bags etc. It is possible that wool and flax for linen were also woven, but this is not mentioned in Young and does not appear to have been practised on a commercial scale. As the 127 weavers must be an underestimate (relying on an individual appearing in the Anglican Parish Registers between 1767 and 1784) and the number of weavers not engaged in producing sailcloth was probably rather slight it is clear that not all such weaving was carried on in the manufactories. Young in 1817 states that the sailcloth manufactories in Whitby contained a total of 109 looms when Whitby was producing about 7,300 bolts a year. He writes that 5000 bolts were produced in 1782 and the figure would likely have been slightly less in 1777; so the probable number of looms in the manufactories in 1777 could have been around 65-70. Even allowing for some degree of shift work, it still seems probable that a significant number of weavers worked from home.

Spinning was not mechanised, and would have been done at home by women. Although the word 'spinster' basically meant someone who did spinning and even in the late 18th Century need not be gender specific, there is no mention to be found in the Whitby parish records of the word referring to anyone other than an unmarried woman. While Whitby would have resounded to the clack of the weaving looms, quiet spinning would have continued relentlessly in any 'free' time for nearly all women in the area who were living below affluence, in order to feed the hungry looms. Not only the sailcloth for ships like *General Carleton* but also that for many of the proud sails of the Royal Navy's ships-of-the-line began with the unrecorded and unrecognised labour of the women and girls of Whitby.

There are 21 mentions in the PR list of people described as sailmakers, which includes both people who owned businesses and those who worked for them. Sail-making

---

[46] *heckling* or *hackling* is a process in flax-dressing in which the flax fibres are pulled through a comb to remove unwanted material.

was a craft that required not only great skill, but also a sizeable loft. Each ship was individual, and *General Carleton* would have been specially measured for her suite of sails by an experienced craftsman; it was important to know the width of the yards and the required length of each sail. A sail that was too long would still be slack in a firm breeze and would not be efficient, too short and it would not fill out sufficiently and could split. Each sail had to be carefully made of a number of pieces of canvas double-stitched together. The edges were reinforced by hemming the edges and by sewing a rope, known as a bolt-rope, at the top and bottom. In spite of all this sails needed constant repair, and had to be replaced every four or five years, so there was a guaranteed regular income if you could get the ongoing contract to supply a ship, and one way to do this was to buy a share. Robert Hunter supplied the sails for *Henrietta* in 1764, and he was still in business when *General Carleton* was built, but either James Atty or William Chapman are perhaps the more likely to have supplied *General Carleton*, as both had Campion connections, and whichever it was could also have been a part-owner of the ship. We have already seen that James Atty was a part-owner of a prodigious number of vessels; in 1787 Robert Hunter was part-owner of seven Whitby ships and William Chapman of six.

A ship such as *General Carleton* would have used an enormous mileage of rope. The bill for rope for *Three Sisters*, *Henrietta* and *Ann* was in the order of two or three times as much as that paid for the sails. With serious money to be made, it is no surprise that Whitby had its own roperies, in the PR list there are 37 ropers. The oldest ropery, a quarter of a mile long, was on the top of what is now called Boulby Bank, and was owned by Thomas Boulby from 1737. This is Adam Boulby's younger brother who married Jane Campion. Thomas Boulby still owned it in 1781 when he appears in Bailey's Directory. There was another ropery, 380 yards long, at Spital Bridge near the Dock Company premises which Young mentions as belonging to Abel Chapman in 1817, so was likely to be in Chapman ownership in 1777 when it was rented by Jonathan Lacy. The third ropery, of 240 yards and on the West side of the river, was owned in 1817 by Henry Goodwill (or Goodel) who also appears in the parish register as a roper in 1770. Benjamin Dove supplied the ropes for *Henrietta*, and he certainly could have done so for *General Carleton*, but I suspect Thomas Boulby was not only the supplier of her rope but was also possibly a part-owner of *General Carleton*. He had all the right connections: he not only married a Campion, but his nephew Robert had married Martha Holt – Nathaniel Campion's sister-in-law. Also Thomas Boulby's elder brother Adam was a kind of patron of Thomas Pyman. The collection of coils of tarred rope in the Polish National Maritime Museum at Gdańsk which was recovered from the *General Carleton* wreck gain added interest when we can imagine them being made at Whitby in the Boulby ropery on the steep east bank above Church Street.

Blocks were another large investment; an 8" single block cost 11½d (£4.48; £57.40), and a 9" double cost 2/7½ (£12.26; £157.22). These were pulley wheels encased in a wooden frame to ensure the ropes did not slide off, and when two or more were used together they were called a *block and tackle* which enabled the seamen to lift weighty objects and manipulate the heavy sails with less effort. Block-making was often combined with being a mast maker, Thomas – and later John – Huntrodes were a well-known firm of block and mast makers. For *Henrietta* Isaac Allanson, listed in Bailey's directory (1781) as a mast maker, provided the blocks, and Mr Linskill the masts.

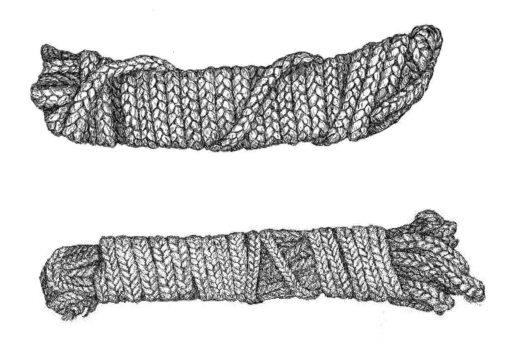

Figs 5a & 5b: Coils of rope from the *General Carleton* wreck, possibly made in Thomas Boulby's ropewalk.

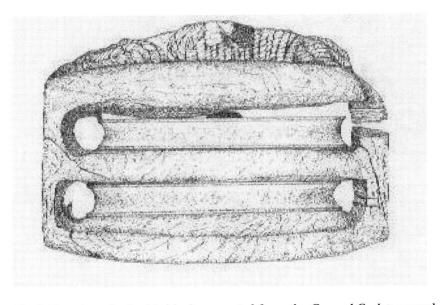

Fig 6: Drawing of a double block excavated from the *General Carleton* wreck.

59

22: Warehouse at Spital Bridge, formerly the site of William Chapman's sailcloth manufactory. It is possible the sails for *General Carleton* were made here.

23. An underwater picture of another of *General Carleton's* bower anchors. It is possible they were made in Whitby by John Brignall, anchorsmith.

24: The best preserved of the jackets found in the *General Carleton* wreck. It is a made of fulled wool, and is typical sailor's jacket of the period, cut short and close-fitting and with sleeves which can be rolled up to make it safe and practicable. This jacket is brown; both brown and blue jackets were common for mariners, though blue seems to have been more popular. The measurements of the jacket indicate that the owner was about 5' 7" which would be about average for a male of the period.

25: Canvas waistcoat, which has been made using sailmaking techniques, possibly by one of the crew.

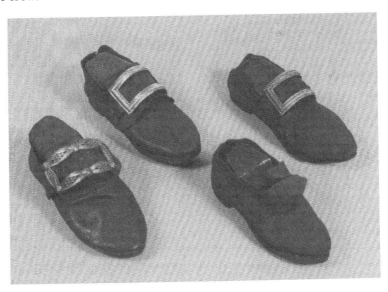

26. Shoes and buckles from *General Carleton*. Shoes would have been one of the items which sailors would have bought ready made.

27: This Fair Isle knitted woollen hat was recovered in almost perfect condition, though the colours have faded. It was a practical garment which would keep the head warm without blowing off in the wind, and the thrum fringe would help keep rain out of the eyes. Sailors often would cover their woollen hats with tar which would make them more weatherproof; however the owner of this beautiful hat clearly did not wish to spoil it by doing that. Maybe it had been knitted as a present from a relative or sweetheart. Jill Goodwin, an authority on vegetable dyeing and the author of A *Dyer's Manual*, has suggested that if the present colours are close to the originals it could have been dyed with walnut (which requires no mordant) or onion skins (which give a range or oranges, browns and yellows), or the darkest colour could be faded madder – if so, the original could have been a rather impressive pattern of red, orange, yellow and natural wool colour. A knitting pattern for this iconic hat can be found in Appendix 4.

28. The *Endeavour* replica in the Pool of London, 1997. *Endeavour* was built as *Earl of Pembroke* in 1764 at Thomas Fishburn's yard for Thomas Millner. She was a 368-ton bark, so slightly smaller than the 370-ton ship *General Carleton*. However, the two vessels would probably have looked very similar with the blunt square bows and rather box-like appearance which are clearly visible in this picture.

Smales' Masting Book exists in the Whitby Lit & Phil, though the firm did not do the masting for *General Carleton*; it seems to have concentrated more on smaller vessels.

Once the masts were fitted and the sails, ropes and blocks were purchased, the ship could be rigged. Specialist riggers in the PR list were John Hall, Charles Noddings and Robert Persith. The rigging for *Henrietta* was done by John Turnbull.

While all this was going on, and *General Carleton* was filled with noises of sawing and hammering, and the smell of wood-shavings and paint, Nathaniel Campion and Thomas Pyman, sometimes with some of the other owners would visit the ship regularly to keep an eye on the progress.

Then there was the crew to appoint, and we know the names of those who sailed on *General Carleton* from the muster rolls. Although the selection of the crew was the decision of the master, he was clearly open to advice and recommendation. Most important was the choice of mate. On board ship the master was all-powerful in his own fiefdom, and his orders were to be obeyed. It was the mate's job to ensure that this was the case. As second in command he needed to be skilled in all the qualities required of a master not only to ensure there was always a competent officer awake at all hours, but also to take over the ship in the event of the master suffering from a debilitating accident or illness, or even dying. The mate for *General Carleton's* maiden voyage was Thomas Adamson. It is a common name; but he was probably the son of William Adamson and Sarah née Jefferson of Staithes. The family was known to the Campions: Thomas' elder brother John was appointed mate of Samuel Campion's ship *Apollo* in 1775, was master of this ship from 1776-1782, and was still master of her in 1787. Thomas had sailed on *Elizabeth* in 1768 and *Speedwell* in 1771 – both ships owned by Thomas Holt, a possible part-owner of *General Carleton*. It is therefore likely that Thomas Pyman was recommended to appoint Thomas Adamson by some of his fellow owners. The 2nd mate was Nicholas Robinson son of Richard, and it is possible he also came with recommendations as, like Adamson, he had sailed on *Speedwell*. There was a young Richard Robinson, perhaps a cousin, who had been a servant on *Speedwell* for some years and in 1777 sailed on her again as a seaman for the first time. Nicholas' son, also Nicholas, was later to sail as a servant on *Diligence*, owned by Isaac Stockton, Thomas Holt's father-in-law. William Taylor was chosen as carpenter on *General Carleton*, and the cook was William Parker.

There were also eight *servants*, or apprentices, who are not named on the muster roll. However, it is possible to have an informed guess as to who they were from the following year's muster roll. They were almost certainly: George Stockton, William Daniel, John Noddings, Robert Dunn, Simon Frankland, Nathaniel Stonehouse, John Featherstone and Isaac Hornby.

Nothing is yet known about Isaac Hornby, but of the others the oldest was George Stockton who sailed from Whitby on his 16th birthday. He was the son of Isaac Stockton who was probably related to the Isaac Stockton who was Thomas Holt's father-in-law. John Featherstone was a day younger than George Stockton, so still only 15 when he sailed. He had previously served on Nathaniel Campion's ship *Valiant* under Thomas Pyman. Nathaniel Stonehouse, 15, was related to Nathaniel Campion by marriage. William Daniel, also 15, was the son of an exciseman. Robert Dunn was 14, as was Simon Frankland who came from Staithes, and whose mariner father William was probably also known to the Campions.

John Noddings was just 12. His mother, Hannah, had no doubt spent time and money ensuring that he was well-equipped for his first day as an apprentice. This would involve him having a seaman's chest. These were of crucial importance as they contained all the property a sailor needed on a voyage, which in some cases was all the property he had, and they were lockable which meant they were the only place where his belongings could be safe. They also served as a seat or table. John's chest would have been bought locally; Whitby was known for making sea chests, usually in a combined kit of *seaman's chests and bedding*, in sufficient quantities not only to supply the town's mariners, but also to export them – mainly to Hull and Newcastle, but also to London.

A surviving document lists articles which were either not returned or returned damaged at Portsmouth Yard from the storeship *Hopkins* in October 1781. It provides useful information about what were considered necessary items at sea, and how much they cost. In terms of bedding, bolsters were 11d, blankets 2/6 (£13.70; £150.40) and coverlets 2/5. It is likely that items of bedding in daily use on *General Carleton* were possibly not stowed away each day and probably perished in the wreck, so the four surviving blankets were extra ones kept safe in the sea-chests; spare blankets were useful items not only to keep warm on chilly Baltic nights, but also as raw material for customising their clothes: Babits and Brenckle suggest that the lining of one of the jackets and one pair of the breeches found in the wreck were made from blanket.

A sailor's most valuable possessions were his clothes, which might include a jacket or two, a waistcoat or two, three shirts, a pair of trousers and a pair of breeches, two pairs of drawers, two or thee pairs of stockings, two pairs of shoes, a couple of handkerchiefs, a pair of mittens, a hat and a cap. Examples of all these were recovered from the wreck of *General Carleton*. The surviving clothes were all from the stern section of the ship, and so are likely to have comprised the contents of the sea-chests of the master, mate, and the servants, possibly the carpenter – in all nine or ten people. Bearing in mind that it is likely that not all the contents of all the chests have survived, and that the crew were also wearing clothes at the time, the number of clothes and parts of clothes which survived (for example, 15 jackets or jacket parts and 27 stockings or stocking parts) suggests that some of those involved may have had had a considerably larger wardrobe. The *Hopkins* document prices *Kersey Jackets* at 7/1, *Linsey Waiscooats* [sic] at 3/- and *Kersey* ones at 5/3, *Kersey Breeches* at 4/9, *Checqu'd Shirts* at 3/6, *Frocks* at 3/5, *Trowsers* at 3/5, *Stockings* at 2/3, *Shoes* at 5/3, *Worsted Caps* at 10d and *Dutch Caps* at 1/8.

If John's mother bought a sea-chest and bedding and a full kitting out of new clothes she would have paid something in the order of £3-5s (£356; £4,000). However, as an apprentice he would also have to run errands when ashore, and spend the winter season living in the Pyman household, so he would also need some shore clothes as well. How much of this was actually bought ready-made from a shop is open to question; it seems unlikely that it all was, as that would have been regarded as a rather pretentious extravagance, and may have resulted in his being teased by the older hands aboard.

Sir Frederick Morton Eden wrote, in his *State of the Poor* that *In the North...almost every article of dress worn by farmers, mechanics, and labourers, is manufactured at home.* Although this was written in 1797 it is, as Styles has pointed out, not to be taken too seriously but is propaganda for his view that the poor are able to live lives of *robust and virtuous self-sufficiency*. What Styles suggests is a more complex pattern where some items: hats, shoes, handkerchiefs and aprons were bought ready-made from a shop, market or peddler. As we have seen spinning was a skill routinely expected of women, those in north east Yorkshire being particularly experienced at spinning flax and hemp. There is evidence from this area that it was common for hempen or flaxen yarn to be spun at home, then sent out to be woven into cloth, which would be made up into coarse shirts and shifts at home.

An expert spinner could spin enough to make more cloth than the household needed, and that was sold on as a lucrative sideline.

Wool was also spun and knitted into stockings; this could be done purely for household use or could also involve making a surplus which could be sold direct or through a middle man. Although the stocking-knitting frame had been invented for some time, it is interesting that fewer than half of the stockings or stocking parts recovered from *General Carleton* were machine made.

It was also the case that household-spun wool was sent out to be woven, but was only rarely made into garments at home; it was more usual to take the cloth to another professional to have it made up into clothes by someone like William Hawkins *breeches maker* who married at Whitby in October 1781. As the cloth from homespun wool was a rather coarse kersey, material for special clothes which required a finely woven cloth was bought and made up perhaps by a tailor, or mantua-maker for women's clothes.

Any of the clothes that were bought would be of local manufacture. In addition to *Seamans Chests and Bedding*, Whitby was exporting *Bedding linen & wearing Apparel*, *worsted Stuffs* and *Worsted stockings* to other coastal ports.

There was a commercial stocking enterprise run by Abraham Dent at Kirby Stephen, part of whose documents have survived. He mainly sold military and naval hose on government contract; but also supplied civilian ware. He supplied a range of products whose price represents the quality and durability. *Sergeants hose* retailed at 31s per dozen, *mariners hose* was the same price as *marching regiments hose* at 13s 6d per dozen, and ordinary *soldiers hose* was 12s per doz. Civilian stockings could cost much more with *men's fine ribbed worsted* costing £2 17s a dozen, *men's fine ribbed yarn* a guinea a dozen, while *ordinary men's* could be bought as cheap as 10s a dozen. Interestingly *blue women's* (which arguably gave their name to the Bluestocking Society) sold for 11s a dozen[47].

Shoes would have been bought, and there were several shoemakers active in Whitby at this period.

Experienced sailors would buy their clothing from specialist slop-shops that could be found near the docks in most ports. Young mentions that in 1816 Whitby had six slop-shops, and there would certainly be some in 1777, with the proprietors of such establishments appearing in the parish records as shop keepers. Many seamen would also be able to make their own clothes, at least of the simpler kind. Whether John Noddings made any of his own clothes, he would certainly be expected to know how to repair them. Into his sea-chest would go needles and thread. Pins, needles, a needle case with a thimble, and a personal sewing kit which included a pair of scissors, a button and fragments of material, were all found in the *General Carleton* wreck.

John Noddings' father, also John, who had paid perhaps £20 (£2,100; £22,000) for his son's seven-year apprenticeship to Pyman, no doubt had lectured him on the fact that at 12 he was no longer a child but had to make his way in the world which involved working hard and concentrating on his learning so that one day he might become a master mariner. He would advise him to respect his elders, obey the captain without demur and avoid swearing, hard liquor and loose women. His father may have given him a book on the art of navigation.

---

[47] Prices given are for 1768-1770. Information from Willan, T S.

**Fig 7: An apprentice on General Carleton darning
one of his stockings. Many of the stockings excavated
showed signs of being mended.**

His mother was born Hannah Sneaton and her father Henry, a carpenter, was the brother of Elizabeth who had married Thomas Pyman's father. It was her family connections that resulted in her cousin Pyman agreeing to take her son John as his, possibly first, apprentice. Hannah's advice perhaps involved advising him to be brave, good and honest, and remember to say his prayers. She may have given him a copy of the Bible and/or a prayer book.

What all three of them knew, but probably did not mention, was that though he would find comradeship and maybe friendship among his fellow apprentices, there would be humiliating and cruel initiations to be undergone, enforced most strictly by those who had most recently been subjected to them. There would also be teasing from all the more experienced members of the crew which could turn to vindictiveness and bullying. Although there was not the brutality on a merchant ship that was found in the Royal Navy, in the Eighteenth Century cruelty was notoriously accepted part of life in all levels of society; du Roi noticed that on *Prince of Wales* in 1776, captained by the *honourable, upright* George Pressick, the *cabin-boys*, by whom he must mean the servants, *are punished by the captain or the first mate at will*, adding that *this happens almost daily*. He betrays the mood of the times by commenting that *these performances are often very comical*.

In the light of this both the young John Noddings and his parents were glad that Thomas Pyman would look after him. This did not mean he would not be given the occasional slap, but the worst elements of the crew would not risk offending the captain by persecuting his cousin, and the more far-sighted might realise that such a well-connected young boy might, in just eight years or so, himself be a master with the power to employ sailors – and making a good impression now could be of benefit in the future.

Among the other possessions that would be packed in John's sea-chest would be a penknife, some spare food (perhaps bacon and cheese), soap, and maybe a toothbrush (an item most sailors would not possess). It would be several years before he would need a shaving brush or razor, as his maturer fellow sailors had[48].

According to the muster roll the master, mate, carpenter, cook and eight servants were entered on *General Carleton* at Whitby on 12 March 1777, and six seamen were enrolled at Hull on 26 April. It would certainly have been possible for Pyman to sail the ship from Whitby to Hull with this rather skeletal crew, but it would have been very unwise with a new vessel and some rather inexperienced apprentices, and I doubt that his fellow owners would have sanctioned it. Though the core crew were on the payroll from 12 March that does not mean the ship sailed on that day – there would be preliminary duties to perform; even so it leaves a question about what was happening between 12 March and 26 April. It has to be remembered that, while muster rolls are crucially important documents, their accuracy can not be relied upon, and this particular muster roll exemplifies this need for caution. Not only does it have *General Carleton* taking a month and a half to sail from Whitby to Hull, it records that the seamen enlisted on 26 April were not discharged until 5 December, in spite of another six men being signed on at London and a further six at Hull on 14 May; the first sailors to be discharged, according to the muster roll, are six seamen set ashore at London on 16 August. If this were the case then the ship would have had a crew of 31 between 14 May and 16 August – a reckless extravagance which would ensure, as the main on-going expenses of a ship were the wages and provisions for the crew, that instead of making a healthy profit to offset the large capital outlay, *General Carleton's* first voyage gratuitously racked up the debt! This is clearly nonsense, especially if the document is examined more closely: it states that the seamen who ostensibly served from 26 April to 5 December were on board for only 1 month and 14 days, and those allegedly embarking on 5 May had only been aboard for 3 months when they disembarked on 5 December.

It seems much more likely that *General Carleton's* first six seamen were entered at Hull on 26 March and discharged on 10 May also at Hull; that the ship sailed from Hull on 14 May with another six seamen who were discharged at London on 16 August, and the final six served between 5 September and 5 December.

Although the six seamen (William Rudd, John Hutchinson, Isaac Raine, John Corner, James Dearey and David Coulson) were entered at Hull, they can all be identified as being local to Whitby. This suggests that they were all on board when *General Carleton* left Whitby though they were working their passage, and their wages were not paid until the voyage officially began when the ship sailed from Hull on 26 March.

So this was the crew who sailed on the maiden voyage of *General Carleton*. She left her moorings on the first tide on a bright March morning, at first towed by a cobble foy through the narrow bridge[49] and out of the harbour and then north-westerly along the

---

[48] A shaving brush and a number of razors were found in the *General Carleton* wreck.

[49] *General Carleton* was 29ft 6ins wide and Whitby's lift-up bridge when raised provided an opening of only 32ft 6ins, this would give a clearance of only about 15 inches on either side.

Whitby Road, a rock-free channel to the open sea. Once in deep water Pyman ordered the helmsman to steer an easterly course, and asked the mate to set sail; Adamson barked out, *Stand by to make sail!* And each man moved to his designated place to await the series of orders that would raise the sails one by one: the topgallants, topsails, the foresail...

> *Lay aloft and loose the mainsail!*
> *Man the tack and sheet!*
> *Let go clewgarnets, buntlines and leechlines!*
> *Let fall!*
> ...
> *Haul taut! Haul out!*

As each sail was set the freshening breeze filled it with the sudden slap and crack of new canvas until *General Carleton* was moving swiftly across a dark sea speckled and streaked with light in the morning sun, beneath a pale sky seared with gulls' cries. In the eyes of the watchers on the cliffs – parents, wives, sweethearts – she diminished to the size of a small boat before vanishing behind Saltwick Nab.

Chapter 6

1778 - 1779
The Baltic Trade

At the beginning of the 18th Century Whitby was getting rich on the coal trade, and the families that were descended from the owners and masters of colliers at that time had become wealthy and established by the 1770s, examples being Coates, Simpson, Barker, Linskill, Skinner, Simpson, Storm, Gibson, Moorsom, Chapman, Holt, Lotherington, Millner, Moorsom, Breckon, Stockton and Lacy.

By the mid century the north-east ports, particularly Newcastle, Whitby and Scarborough, had dominated the trade at the expense of the southern and south-eastern ports, particularly Ipswich. And among this trio Whitby was exceptional. As the century moved towards its close Whitby was to overtake its early rival Scarborough as a ship-owning port by 1788, becoming the seventh largest port in terms of tonnage of ships owned; and by 1790-91 Whitby was the third largest ship-building port after London and Newcastle, building a sizeable proportion of the tonnage owned at both of these ports. Hull was fourth with a little over two thirds of Whitby's tonnage, and after that Liverpool (the rising port of the 19th Century) lagging in 5th place with not much more than half of Whitby's total, and Bristol came 9th with only a fraction over a quarter.

Many reasons have been suggested for this change, such as the glut of captured Dutch ships flooding the market in the south, and the comparative cheapness of wages and materials in the North-East. This is no doubt the case, but two vital factors which are important but rarely appear in academic journals are the resourcefulness and enterprise of the shipowners, and the skill of Whitby sailors. The North Sea was colloquially referred to as the *nursery of seamen*, and Deane tells us that when Nelson was given command of *Agamemnon* he specifically requested that his connections in the North East should send him sailors from Whitby and Newcastle.

The most significant reason for the predominance of Whitby was in the nature of ship design; as Ralph Davis puts it, the shipyards of the north-east coast were *almost monopolising the building of bulk-cargo carriers* which he describes as involving *the abandonment of fine lines, and coming closer to the shape of the oblong box which will –at its own pace- carry more than anything else contained within the same dimension.* These ships could take almost any cargo anywhere even, because they were virtually flat-bottomed, beaching on a sandy shore fully loaded. And if the stern was narrow (*pinked* ie pinched) they would not be as slow as is sometimes suggested. Du Roi, sailing on the Whitby-built *Prince of Wales*, commented that *the English...make the front part of the vessel broader than the rear part, and this from mature experience, taken from nature,* namely that *the fish, that is the dolphin, which can swim the fastest has been equipped by nature with a big head in proportion to the breadth of his body.*

This gave them enormous flexibility, and Whitby shipowners took advantage, changing - as the opportunities for profit presented themselves - what most people would have thought of as a humble collier into a transport ship or a whaling ship or even a research vessel observing the transit of Venus and searching for the mythical southern continent.

The coal trade was less attractive to Whitby shipowners as the century progressed: in 1755, as John Gould has shown, Whitby-owned ships accounted for nearly a quarter of all coal ships cleared from Newcastle, putting it ahead of all its rivals (followed by Scarborough, then Shields) but by 1789 Whitby had dropped to 4th place (Shields was first, followed by London, then Yarmouth), with less than 7% of the total clearances.

The coal trade had been a convenient one for Whitby, itself a significant consumer of coal especially for the alum trade, as the home port was on the main shipping route from Shields/Newcastle/Stockton/Sunderland to London, East Anglia and the south-east ports. There were agents and factors at each end of the voyage, such as the afore-mention William Jefferson hostman of Newcastle, and William Ward coal-factor of London who was, by 1787, part-owner of eleven Whitby ships[50]. Coal as a cargo was difficult to damage: it was not seriously affected by water or salt, and had no sell-by date, so there was no need to sail without a full hold.

The drawback of the coal-trade was that the master, acting for the owners, had to purchase the coal in Newcastle and sell it in London. This took time. At the Newcastle end this involved the vessel mooring at Shields, the master hiring a horse and riding to Newcastle and negotiating prices with various hostmen; the successful dealer would then arrange for the coal from the agreed mine to be loaded onto boats called *keels* which would be sailed or rowed down to Shields where the coal would be shovelled onto the ship with the seller and the buyer both checking that the right amount had been loaded. Then master and hostman would ride back to Newcastle to pay all the various dues and sign the appropriate paperwork. As we have seen from Ralph Jackson's diary, this process was combined with a certain amount of entertaining, shopping and sightseeing which no doubt helped pass the time; but nonetheless it was a lengthy process, and time was money.

At the other end, with the annual arrival of about 1,500 laden colliers in London in 1755, rising by about another 1,000 by 1790, and the bulk of these arrivals squeezed into some eight or nine months of the year, it was serious chaos as they all sought to unload and sell their wares. Vessels were crammed into the Thames and accidents were common, for example in the Pool of London on 3 April 1755 *John and Elizabeth* of Whitby, master Thomas Holt, *fell across the Hawse* of *Prince Frederick*, Robert Hudson, probably also a Whitby ship. The bowsprit of the latter dislodged the longboat of the former from its chocks and knocked down Moses Sleightholm the cook and Hans Fanna an apprentice. They were attended on shore by the surgeon William Martin who submitted a bill for £6-10s (£940; £10,000) *for attendance and Curing them.*

The master would then have to sell the cargo, on behalf of the owners, at the coal market at Billingsgate, where in addition to the complications owing to the fact that he had bought the coal in Newcastle chaldrons, which was a weight of 53 cwt, and had to sell it in London chaldrons, which was a volume of 36 bushels (weighing about 27cwt), the money he got was subject to the ever-fluctuating price of coal. When a large number of ships arrived in a short space of time, and this was especially the case in wartime when they would travel in convoy, the prices in London would fall accordingly.

And the coal trade was a one-way business; nearly all colliers returning to Newcastle were empty, which means they had to purchase ballast. This was an additional cost in time and money: in 1765 *Henrietta* paid 15d per ton for ballast, and 6s 6d per 20 tons for it to be loaded (*Ballast heaving*). In April she loaded 90 tons, but only 60 in August/September.

---

[50] *Antelope, Brilliant, Christopher, Content, Elizabeth & Ann, Isabella, Midsummer Blossom, Nautilus, Union, Volunteer & Welcome Messenger.*

Ballasting on the Thames was controlled by Trinity House, and the profits made went towards the support of *poor decayed merchant seaman and their widows, who are incapable of labour*. Many sailors and their widows had recourse to these funds, which involved submitting a Trinity House Petition.

Delays, unforeseen costs and an unfavourable price offered in London could make the whole journey into a loss-making exercise. *Three Sisters* made six coal voyages in 1766 and seven in 1767, of these thirteen voyages three made a loss. The total profit for the two years was £51-14-1 (£59,300). James Atty, who owned one sixty-fourth part of the ship received a meagre 18s 7d (£100; £1,100) as his share of the two-year profits. As a ship-owner this is not great wealth; however as a sailmaker he put in a bill for £53-12s (£64,000) for work done!

Most of the other shipping trades involved arranging a fixed freight rate with a merchant for carrying goods from place to place, which clearly had its advantages. This was one of the factors that led to the developing popularity of the Baltic trade among Whitby shipowners. The main ports concerned were: Memel (Klaipėda), in Prussian control, was possibly the most popular Baltic destination for Whitby ships, partly because of its comparative nearness and cheapness compared to Riga, but also because, according to the *Encyclopaedia Britannica* (1815 edition) it boasted *the finest harbour in the Baltic*. Memel's impressively large-scale saw-mills were financed and run by British merchants, and timber had become an efficiently-run specialised export. A document in the National Archives lists all the British ships trading with Memel in 1787. In total 388 ships are recorded of which 49 (12.6%) are from Whitby. The average turn-round time for the 55 recorded visits of Whitby ships where the arrival and departure date are given -and are legible- is a fortnight.

Petersburg, although not 100 years old, had already become a flourishing trading port, and was the second most popular destination for Whitby ships trading in the Baltic. Riga and Narva, both at that time also under Russian influence, supplied timber, flax and hemp, as did Petersburg. Britain had the right sort of ships available in sufficient numbers, so they effectively had a monopoly on trade with Russia, and Whitby, one of England's leading ports in ship-building and ship-owning, was heavily involved in this trade. Riga, the third most popular Baltic port for Whitby vessels, was particularly known for its masts. In January 1780 John Knaggs, master of the hired Whitby ship *William and Mary* arrived at the Government shipyard at Deptford and delivered a cargo of timber and 100 masts of various sizes of which the majority are specifically designated as being from Riga.

William Spavins, seaman on the merchant ship *Elizabeth and Mary*, sailed from Hull to Narva in 1754. He described the port as *a large town bordering on the gulf of Finland whose principle exports were flax, timber and corn*, adding, *There is a remarkable waterfall at some distance above the town, where the river being upwards of a hundred yards wide, the water falls perpendicularly down a rock about twelve feet; the noise whereof may be heard at many miles distant. Above the water-fall is a grand Saw-mill, where timber being floated down the river is stopped, and sawn into beams, planks or deals, and then launched into the river below, and towed down the sea to be taken on board the ships in the road.* It was clearly an impressive sight, and must have similarly impressed the crew of *General Carleton* when they moored at Narva in the summer of 1779.

Danzig (Gdańsk) had a long history as a port and supplied mainly timber. It seems to have been a particularly popular port for smaller Whitby ships, such as the 140-ton *Essay*, Stonehouse, and the 100-ton *Juno*, Roundtree, which were both trading with Danzig in 1778. In the probate inventory of the Whitby shipbuilder William Coulson (1750) *Dantswick plank* is the only part of his sizeable timber store which is identified by its place of origin. It must have been of high quality and favoured by shipbuilders as in 1787 the brothers George and Nathaniel Langborne were importing *deals* and *staves* from Danzig for their shipbuilding business direct to Whitby in their own newly-built 121-ton brigantine *Hilda*, James Watt. *Industry*, David Eunson (owned by William Frank) was also trading between Danzig and Whitby carrying *plank, deals, staves* and *spruce beer*. Whitby was also re-exporting spruce beer: *Flying Fish*, James Patton, shipping *8 Galls* [gallons] *Spruce Beer* to London as part of a shipment for Henry Walker Yeoman and others.

Spruce beer was a refreshing low alcohol drink flavoured with spruce. Jane Austen mentions it in her novel *Emma*, and it is likely that she herself on occasion drank spruce beer which had been exported from Danzig. It was particularly popular with the army as it refreshed the troops without making them drunk; General Amhurst had his special recipe for it. It was customary to add spruce beer and sugar to the rum rations for the troops, this was colloquially known as *swizzle*; the 17th Regiment in 1760 had their own *Swizzle Club*. It was also popular to supply spruce beer to sailors to lower the level of intoxication and consequently raise the effectiveness of the crew, and thereby the safety of the ship. In 1764 *Henrietta* took on board *a Cag of Spruce Beer* for 4s in addition to *Two Casks of Beer & an Anker of Ale* for £1 6s, presumably for the seamen aboard.

Stockholm exported much-needed iron for Britain's burgeoning industrial revolution, and also tar. Tar was essential on board ship not just for rope, but for preserving virtually anything that needed to be waterproofed; tarring was a regular shipboard task, with sailors and their clothes being *daub'd with pitch and tar*[51] which is why seamen were referred to as *tars*. Sailors sometimes made their own hats, known as *tarpaulins*, from tarred canvas; the only known surviving 18th Century example is the one excavated from the wreck of *General Carleton*, fittingly preserved in tar. Swedish pine tar was particularly prized, *Henrietta* buying *a Cask of Stockholm Tar* for 17 guilders, or just under a pound (£113; £1,243), in Memel in 1764. Stockholm was *General Carleton's* final port of call.

For most of her career *General Carlton* traded with Russia, Norway and the Baltic ports, and she may have been designed with this trade in mind. The majority of her cargo on these voyages would have been timber, and it is possible that she had loading ports in the bow for long pieces of wood, especially masts, and which might also have facilitated the loading of the iron bars at Stockholm. *Earl of Pembroke*, the ship that later became James Cook's *Endeavour*, was built with just such a timber port.

Muster rolls only name the place a ship visited when there is a change of crew or in cases of accident or death; and sometimes are even less informative than that – *General Carleton's* muster roll for 1777, as mentioned before, in places is clearly a work of fiction, and her 1778 muster gives no place names at all. However, combining information from a range of sources, we can piece together something of the voyages of *General Carleton* in these years.

When *General Carleton* left Whitby 1777 she went to Hull. Hull was to become her main base for these years of trading with the Baltic, as Newcastle seems to have been the base for *Valiant*. Unlike Whitby, Hull had access to a massive area of the North and Midlands by river and through the increasing network of canals. There was an enormous and growing demand for imported goods, particularly raw materials, and a flourishing export of

---

[51] This is a quotation from the satiric verse of the amateur Whitby poet Twisleton. His verses seem not to have survived apart from extracts Gaskin records. I suspect he may be John Twisleton the roper, in which case he would know about pitch and tar.

manufactured items through Hull. The main import was timber which was a bulk cargo and the exports took up comparatively little space, so most ships sailing to the Baltic went in ballast: hardly any of the Whitby ships sailing to Memel in 1787 carried any cargo, and in those few cases it was additional to ballast. Hull only had 8 ships[52] making 10 journeys, on four of these journeys they had an outward cargo instead of ballast, namely casks of ale – specified as *Burton Ale* in one instance. After the 5 May all Hull ships were in ballast, which suggests that the early Hull ships were taking advantage of the stockpiles of barrels of beer which had been shipped down the Trent and accumulated in warehouses in Hull over the winter months.

Timber had the advantage of being in constant demand, and accounted for about half of all the imports into England at this time. Although the value of the timber imports was only some 3% of the country's total, that was not an issue for the shipowners involved in the trade as they were assured of a regular business with full ships; indeed a third of the cost of timber in Britain was the transport. As the Baltic trade was dominated by British ships, there were a number of agents and factors to arrange contracts, and payment could be done through bills of exchange and letters of credit. Memel had a thriving English community, and even had an English church which continued to serve a congregation into the early 20th Century.

As it was wartime, merchant ships would travel in convoy. The problem with this is that a convoy had to travel at the speed of the slowest vessel. If you were master of the slowest vessel this was tough: you would be harried and bullied, occasionally fired at, sometimes towed, certainly cajoled into setting more sail than was wise – a full press of sail in a strong wind achieved increased speed at the risk of splitting a mast. Sometimes you would simply be left behind. *General Carleton*, as a fine new ship, would have been comparatively speedy, and Pyman would have resented being held back. The price for the freightage of goods would have been pre-arranged so, unlike in the coal trade, the sudden influx of goods when the convoy arrived would not have reduced the money acquired. However, it would have resulted in accidents and delays and higher prices for goods and services purchased while in harbour. Additionally if the master wished to discharge his crew on arrival and enter a new crew when about to leave, a common money-saving practice, there would have been a large number of ships competing to employ the best sailors.

It is likely that Thomas Pyman, sailing in a convoy from the Baltic to Hull, left the rest of the ships and went first to Whitby where he could purchase food and supplies cheaper and more easily from tradesmen with whom he was used to doing business. He probably also discharged his original six seamen, and took on replacements. These were Francis Rowntree, John Douthwait, John Grey, John Atkinson, Jacob Francis and John Couling (whom I have not been able to identify). Atkinson was probably the oldest at 33; Gray the youngest at 21; the other three were all fairly recently married. Intriguingly three of them had previously sailed on *Royal Briton*, owned by John Holt, part-owner of *General Carleton*: Jacob Francis as a servant between 1762-66, the other two as seamen - John Gray briefly in 1771, and John Atkinson in 1775.

Though they joined the ship at Whitby, they were not officially on the payroll until after *General Carleton* had sailed to Hull and was ready to set out to the Baltic once more with the convoy on 14 May. By the 19th she was at Elsinore where ships had to pay their

---

[52] Of these eight ships, five were foreign-built and none built at Hull itself. The largest of these vessels was *Two Brothers* which had seven owners of which four were from Whitby: Joseph Barker, Thomas Middleton, William Reynolds and John Easterby.

dues to pass through the Sound. On the 27th she was at Riga, and that is where Francis Rowntree died – we learn from the muster roll that he *Fell from the main Shrouds in Riga bay & was Drownded.* It was about a fortnight since his young wife Susannah had waved him goodbye from the quayside at Whitby.

It is often assumed that the open sea was the danger zone for sailors; but in fact many accidents and deaths occurred while a ship was in harbour. Nathaniel Campion's brother Jacky had drowned at Riga in 1754[53].

General Carleton possibly made another Baltic voyage before we catch up with her again at London on the 16 August where she discharged her sailors and her cargo. It is possible she had some kind of repairs there, as a new crew were not signed on until 5 September; perhaps it was time spent waiting for the convoy to assemble. On 13 September she was at Elsinore bound for the Baltic once more, and there seems to have been one more trip to Riga before she returned home at the end of the season, passing Elsinore on 5 November. She was in London on 1 December and the whole crew, according to the muster roll, were discharged on 5 December at London. As the six seamen had been recruited in London three months earlier, it seems likely that they were discharged there; but I doubt if *General Carleton* overwintered in London, so there was probably a run up to Whitby which did not find its way onto the muster roll.

It would have been Thomas Pyman's unhappy duty, when they arrived back at Whitby to seek out Susannah Rowntree from among the expectant crowd on the quayside and break the news that her husband was drowned over six months previously. She must have been devastated. As Frances had only officially worked for thirteen days, there would only have been thirteen days' pay, maybe £1-10s (£1,250). In addition she would receive her husband's chest with its contents – very much the sort of personal articles: comb, shaving brush, razor, penknife and clothing which were later recovered from the wreck. This may not seem much in today's acquisitive consumer society, but it would be a sizeable proportion of Francis' actual possessions, and would have had a real value for Susannah. William Wordsworth in his poem *The Sailor's Mother* has the eponymous woman telling her story:

> *I had a son, who many a day*
> *Sailed on the sea; but he is dead;*
> *In Denmark he was cast away;*
> *And I have travelled far as Hull to see*
> *What clothes he might have left, or other property*

In the Royal Navy it was customary for the crew to have an auction of a dead sailor's clothes for the benefit of his widow, and, if he was well-liked his colleagues would bid high, so there would be a bit extra. It is not clear if this was common in the merchant navy where there may not have been sufficient members of crew to make an auction profitable but it is possible that it happened in this case.

Susanna was childless, but in later years she remedied this, though she clearly did not wish to be married again. She had an illegitimate son called Snowdon (presumably the father's surname) in 1780 who died the following year, and an illegitimate daughter Susanna in 1781.

---

[53] Thomas Pyman's son Thomas would also drown in Riga Bay, in 1796 at the age of only 23.

Fig 8: *General Carleton* returns to Whitby. View from Coffee House End.

Over wintering did not mean that a ship was just moored up and left until she was ready to sail again. The ship had to be unrigged, the sails mended if necessary and stowed, and the topmasts struck. Nathaniel Campion, Thomas Pyman and possibly William Taylor, the carpenter, would have thoroughly inspected the ship, making a note of what repairs were needed, and what recaulking was required. An inventory would have been made of the ship's equipment, identifying articles which needed mending or replacing. The ship would be beached and at low tide her undersides cleared of barnacles and other accretions, and the timberwork inspected and minor repairs to the hull carried out. *Three Sisters* ran up a bill of £76-10-3½ (£88,000) for winter disbursements at Whitby in 1777, but that was largely because she was a fairly old ship, and was having a major work done by Henry Barrick and Co which involved being brought *in to the Dock*. Her other expenses included 10/6 to Gideon Ward for *attending the Ship*, 9 guineas for *a New Boate* and £11-19s for *the Muster role*.

In the longer run Pyman and Campion would have to plan for the next year in terms of finding cargoes, purchasing supplies and recruiting seamen.

29: View from the outer harbour showing Whitby's eighteenth-century bridge. Print engraved by E Finden from a picture by W Westall.

30: Whitby outer harbour today, looking across to the east bank, the modern bridge is just visible.

For sailors the winter months could be something of a holiday to compensate for having to work seven days a week while at sea. However, this rather depended whether they were prudent with the money they had earned: drinking and gambling were notoriously common among the population at large in the 18th Century, and sailors were considered to be among the worst offenders. Pyman would have actively discouraged drunkenness aboard, and may even have run a *dry ship*, but there were opportunities for drinking while in foreign ports and, once back home, Whitby with seventy or more alehouses[54] provided plenty of scope for expensive alcoholic excesses; as for gambling it would have been common aboard *General Carleton* –indeed a dice cup was found among the salvaged artefacts. For many a sailor's family the household budget had been exhausted by the time the sailing season started again.

Fig 9: **Dice cup, made of horn, from the *General Carleton* shipwreck.**

However, Thomas Pyman was not in this category. A master was comparatively well paid, and I doubt if Pyman drank or gambled his money away. In 1777 John Galilee, Master of *Three Sisters* received £64 (£73,600) for the year's voyages. This was a standard rate of pay which had been the same since 1761, whereas the seamen's wages rose in wartime and slumped in the years of peace depending upon demand, varying from 25% of what the master was paid to over 60%. However, in addition to his pay the master of a ship received perks and various *allowances* or customary bonuses and gratuities which could greatly enhance his take-home pay. Pyman, as part-owner, would also have had his share of the profits.

Thomas Pyman would have returned to his family home at West Cliff with his wife Esther, his ten-year-old daughter Mary, his seven-year-old daughter Esther and his four-year-old boy Thomas, spending the winter in the way that Defoe describes master mariners: as living *calm and secure with their families…enjoying plentifully, what in summer they got*

---

[54] A list of alehouse keepers for 1788 lists 84, 10 called the *Ship*, two with no sign, and five with no name listed; so it is difficult to know if there are some duplicates. The *Cargo Landed* was run by a George Littlefair, who may have been related to the servant of the same name who sailed on *General Carleton*.

laboriously at sea. However, it must be remembered that Thomas would have had his servant John Noddings, and perhaps other servants, lodging in the house and would have had to teach him about navigation and the mathematics involved.

Eighteenth-century Whitby, like all towns with pretensions to fashion, had a coffee house, which was on the west bank at the end of Haggersgate. It overlooked the recently developed quay which Young described as *commodious* and forming, with the West Pier, *a most excellent promenade.* At the coffee house the masters and shipowners would regularly assemble to discuss matters of business and pleasure, to make contacts and contracts, and to read the papers. There would certainly be *Lloyds' List* there, which would enable shipowners to keep a track of the vessels in which they had a financial interest. There would be other journals in which they could follow the war news which was varied. As with all wars, reports were often rather tendentious, with each side making often mutually contradictory claims and assertions about the dreadful conduct of the enemy; the British press claiming that *The Rebels are worse than Savages* and the American papers waxing lyrical about *the Brutal cruelties of the British Troops and their bloody mercenaries* who, among a catalogue of other alleged war crimes, *ravish Virgins before the Eyes of their Parents.*

However some news was reported accurately. In July 1777 General Howe, with 15,000 troops sailed from New Jersey all the way up to the north end of Chesapeake Bay in difficult weather where they landed at the Elk River in late August. Howe's fleet of 265 ships included a large number of transport and supply ships, many of which would have been Whitby vessels: we know that *Royal George*, J Kneeshaw (carrying soldiers from the 37th Foot Regiment); *Eagle*, T Noble (Queen's American Rangers); *Hunter*, J Hodgson (71st Regiment); *Ocean*, J Tindall, and *Argo*, George Tate (New Jersey Volunteers) were there. Charles Walker of Scarborough, on board the transport *Sea Venture*, made his will while at Elk River, leaving all his property to his son Daniel who unfortunately inherited within the year.

After defeating General Washington at the battle of Brandywine Creek on 11 September, Howe led his troops unopposed into Philadelphia on the 26th. As it was the home of the Continental Congress and therefore the capital of the nascent American republic, Howe possibly thought that capturing Philadelphia would end the war. He was mistaken, as Napoleon was to make a similar mistake with Moscow in 1812. Taking Philadelphia was at the expense of supporting the campaign of General Burgoyne who, even after he knew that Howe could provide him with no assistance, relentlessly and recklessly pursued his plans unchanged by circumstances. Among the captured troops when General Burgoyne surrendered at Saratoga were the troops of Hesse-Cassel and Brunswick including Lieutenant du Roi.

In the spring of 1778 *General Carleton* set off, presumably from Whitby, with the same master, mate, carpenter and cook as before. William Rudd had risen from seaman to 2nd mate. John Corner, seaman in 1777, was back again; but otherwise there were two new sailors: Thomas Thompson and John Wells.

There were also four new apprentices: Thomas Harrison, John Tolamy, George Littlefair and Zacharias Campion. Zacharias was the son of Thomas, fisherman of Staithes, and first cousin of Nathaniel Campion to whom Zacharias was doubtless apprenticed.

The muster roll shows that the entire crew served from 4 April to 14 September, but gives no idea where the crew were entered or discharged, or of where she visited between these dates. The late start and the early finish suggest the Baltic trade as the harsh winter there and the brackish water meant that it was icebound for several months each year.

81

However once again the muster roll is misleading, as the Hull port book[55] shows *General Carleton* arriving there on 14 October 1778, one month after the date given for the end of her sailing season. *General Carleton* had in fact come from Onega with a cargo of fir timber, deals and battens shipped for Ralph Dodsworth, and deals and six small masts for Maister.

Onega was a Russian White Sea port with a flourishing timber trade largely in the hands of English merchants who had acquired the right to fell trees, and who were soon to build their own saw-mills. This meant that business could be transacted in English which would be a real bonus – even though masters would of necessity pick up a handful of useful phrases in a number of languages in the areas they regularly traded, and English-speaking factors would be quite common in ports when the British ships visited. The trading season with Onega was short as, like the Baltic, it was ice-bound in winter but, as the Norwegian Coast continued to be navigable because of the Gulf Stream, it was common for ships that sailed to the Baltic or White Sea ports to do additional voyages to Norway at the beginning and the end of the season.

The unreliability of *General Carleton's* muster rolls suggests that Pyman had left the job to the mate. Possibly Pyman did find the mate wanting, because in 1779 he replaced Thomas Adamson, who had been so strongly supported by some of the other owners, with Thomas Williamson, no doubt a choice of his own, and possibly a relative of his wife's. Williamson remained mate on *General Carleton* so long as Pyman was master, and was later mate on Pyman's own ship *Peggy*. Otherwise the crew remained much the same. William Rudd had gone, as had the position of 2nd mate; of the four seamen, three had sailed on *General Carleton* before, the new man was William Hebron.

William Hebron's life is of interest; in 1760 at the age of 32 he was mate on *Speedwell*, John Tayler (Thomas Holt owner) and five years later he was master of the same ship. However, although he clearly could do a mate's job well, he apparently was not up to being master; so far as is known he was never appointed master again but was mate on a number of ships: *Royal Briton*, with John Holt both owner and master, *Dorothy & Catherine*, Isaac Campion, Nathaniel's younger brother (owner Robert Galilee) and in 1776 on Nathaniel Campion's *Valiant*, Richard Thompson. After that time illness, disability or age apparently made him unable to fulfil the duties of mate. It is possible that his being a seaman on *General Carleton* was an act of charity, or possibly with the wartime shortage of good sailors, he was signed on as a man who knew the job and could be relied on, even though he was already 50. In 1787, at the age of 58, he was still working - as cook on *Recovery*, owned by Samuel Campion, Nathaniel's elder brother. It looks as if the Campion family knew, respected and liked William Hebron, and tried to do their best for him. William Hebron's wife Elizabeth died in 1797 aged 72 and he died fifteen years later at the age of 82; how they supported themselves in their long old age can only be imagined.

Other changes in the 1779 crew were that Tolemy was no longer a servant; nor was Littlefair, though he was to be in the crew again in 1780. Thomas Harrison had been replaced by Andrew Harrison, and Isaac Hornby by Thomas Hornby. There were two other new servants: John Johnson and Richard Trueman.

Richard Trueman was a new apprentice and very young, possibly not quite twelve years old when he boarded *General Carleton* in 1779. He lived in Robin Hood's Bay (which was known as *Robinhoods Town* or *Baytown*) and had made his way to Whitby, by boat or

---

[55] The Port Books list all the dutiable cargoes exported and imported. Those for Whitby are mainly in good condition. Those for Hull are more variable. The London Port Books were destroyed.

carrier's cart, with his new chest of clothes, bedding and personal effects. A lad of 12 was expected to earn his own keep, though his apprenticeship would have been paid for by his father Christopher. His parents must have been apprehensive at saying goodbye to their young son, committing him to a life at sea in wartime. In the event Richard was to be one of the longest serving crewmen on *General Carleton*, and was in his final year of apprenticeship when the ship went down in 1785. It is almost certain that some of his possessions are now in the Maritime Museum at Gdańsk.

On 21 March 1779, before *General Carleton* had even set sail from Hull, there was another loss: William Parker, the cook, died *Occasioned by a Violent Cold Rec'd* [received] *on board*. Perhaps he had been acting as caretaker of the ship. Within five days Pyman had found a replacement, James Watson, and two days later they sailed for the Baltic in convoy.

Chapter 7

The War Comes to Yorkshire

On 21 April 1778 John Paul Jones, a privateer supported by the French, landed with a body of men at Whitehaven from *Ranger* under an American flag with the intention of burning all the ships in port. This was the last invasion on English soil, but there was no reason to think this would be the case at the time. Britain was used to invasions and invasion scares. The Dutch had captured the Isle of Sheppey in 1660, and in 1667 had launched the largest military landing in England since mediaeval times at Languard point near Harwich. More recently, and within living memory of some, would have been the fears of a successful invasion by French and Spanish in support of the Jacobite Rebellion of 1715. Invasion panic surged again in 1744 when the French mustered troops at Dunkirk planning to land at Maldon and march on London to make Charles Edward Stuart king. France had planned another assault in 1756, and in 1759 an even more ambitious scheme was formulated in which France, Russia, Sweden and Holland would provide troops to land simultaneously in Scotland and Essex. The fact that none of these came to anything did not make the fear of invasion any less real.

However, to call Jones' attack on Whitehaven an invasion is something of an exaggeration. It was never intended as any more than a raid; indeed a punitive raid, as Jones had a personal agenda. He had started his career as a sailor as a 12-year-old lad at Whitehaven, and had risen swiftly to be a mate. His style of discipline was rather too rigorous and over-zealous even for those harsh times and there was an incident in which Jones struck a member of the crew, a native of Whitehaven, who died. After that he could no longer find employment in Whitehaven and he was driven out in disgrace; now was payback time.

The sortie started well; with some of his men John Paul Jones managed to seize the forts overlooking the harbour, tie up the guards and spike the guns. The rest of his invasion force went straight to a dockside inn. Jones eventually fetched them out but then discovered that they had landed with no incendiary materials, and had to borrow some from the generous local inhabitants who had no idea that the town was being invaded. Even so, they made a mess of the arson and only one vessel was partly burnt. The alarm was raised and Jones with the rest of the men made a tactical withdrawal.

It is clear that most of his crew, all of whom were British born, had no great political agenda but were looking for an easy life and much plunder; but it is undeniable that the incident had an enormous impact throughout the country, and that a major propaganda victory had been won. John Paul Jones had brought a distant war uncomfortably close to home; and no-one who lived near the coast could sleep with the cosy reassurance of safety that they had before.

France had happily been exploiting the situation raised by the American Independence war. England was France's *hereditary enemy*, and England's misfortunes were opportunities for France to discomfort Britain and perhaps to gain some of the losses she had suffered during the Seven Years' War. To begin with she had sponsored men like Jones, and American privateers wrought some damage on Whitby trade. On Friday 25 July 1777 Captain Barker of the Whitby ship *Mary* arrived at Hull with news of four ships captured off the Yorkshire coast by the American Privateer *Pegasus*, Richard Allen, which had 16 carriage guns and a crew of over 100 men - a third of whom were Irish and the rest French. On Saturday 2 August Anthony Watson arrived back in Whitby to tell that *Thomas and Elizabeth*, of which he was master, returning from St Petersburg with a cargo of deals and iron had been captured by the 26-gun American privateer *Tartar*, Grimes. Anything valuable was taken on board *Tartar*, and the ship was scuttled. Whitby responded by repairing the half moon battery which guarded the harbour entrance, and equipping it with eight 32-pounders.

In June 1778 France joined the war, now convinced by the surrender of General Burgoyne at Saratoga that the Americans had a serious army, and things became even more difficult. French privateers became bolder, one trying to capture a ship returning from Archangel even as it was sailing towards Whitby harbour. The ship retaliated, as did the guns from Whitby's newly refurbished battery, and the privateer gave up. One French privateer was bold enough to come ashore near Whitby to steal sheep.

However, the enemy did not have it all their own way. *Jane* of Sunderland was captured by the enemy; but afterwards was taken back from them by the Whitby ship *Hannah*, commanded by Captain Fleck.

The British war policy had been to focus on the more rebellious north of America, concentrating its forces in a comparatively restricted area, and seeking to capture all the significant ports from New York to Canada with the aim of destroying their trade and ruining their economy, thus rendering the Americans unable to continue the war. Newport was captured by the British in 1777, a number of Whitby ships being involved in taking troops, supplies and provisions to support this campaign including *Esk*, (304 tons); *Father's Goodwill*, (333); *Lord Sandwich*, John Blanchard, (368); *Rachel & Mary*, Francis Rowbotham, (320), and *Saville*, William Hustler (355).

All this changed with the entry of the French into the war. The war ceased to be focussed simply in America, but moved into areas of contention between Britain and France, notably the West Indies. Also the British policy had relied on having almost effortless control of the sea, but the prospect of French warships off the American coast made re-thinking their strategy imperative.

In the summer of 1778 there was a plan for a combined attack on the British at Newport, with the French attacking by sea and the Americans by land. To prevent the French from landing, or being able to anchor sufficiently near the shore for the town to be within range of their cannon, the British sank a number of transports of which two had been used as prison ships: *Rachel and Mary* and *Lord Sandwich*. Both these were Whitby-built vessels. *Rachel and Mary* was still owned at Whitby; *Lord Sandwich* was Cook's *Endeavour*[56].

Saville, William Hustler, had returned from Rhode Island and was safely at Deal, bound for *the River* [Thames] on 23 May. This was the last time he sailed on *Saville*; in January 1779 he was master of Nathaniel Campion's *Valiant*.

In the event the French ships were caught in a storm and decided to go to Boston for repairs before attacking Newport, this left the American land forces attacking on their own, and they were eventually defeated. Newport was reinforced; in March 1778 *Argo*, George Tate, was busy taking troops of the 10th, 21st, 33rd, 53rd, 62nd and 71st regiments from the

---

[56] We know this and much more about transport ships and Newport in the Revolutionary War from the exhaustive research carried out by Dr Kathy Abbass Director of the Rhode Island Marine Archaeology Project.

frigate *Orpheus* anchored at Cape Cod to Rhode Island. By November 1778 thirty-nine of the eighty British transports in America were based at Rhode Island. Clearly they were taking no chances; the threat from the French navy continued, and the fiercely independent Rhode Islanders were proving hard to control as they were inalienably wedded to their rights of life, liberty and the pursuit of smuggling.

The weather may have helped the British at Newport, but on the east coast of Britain the winter of 1778-9 was terrible. In late December a hurricane caused massive devastation in the north-east: several ships were wrecked, many with loss of life, including *Four Brothers* of Whitby, the master, Jackson, and eight crew members drowned. The Norfolk coast also suffered, with many vessels and houses damaged or destroyed and fields flooded with a great loss of livestock. The fierce weather continued; in early January as the whaling fleet was being re-fitted in the harbour, part of Whitby abbey was blown down, which many would have regarded as a bad omen.

But Yorkshiremen are stout-hearted and stubborn, rising to the challenge of adversity, and when the nine whalers sailed out of Whitby harbour on Wednesday 17 February 1779 for the Davis Straits it was an impressive sight. All the ships were well armed and *stoutly manned*, all their masters had made an agreement of mutual aid and to act as a fleet, under the command of Thomas Franks, master of *Marlborough*, which had most guns and a letter of marque registering her as a privateer. The other ships were *Addison*, James Banks; *Friendship*, George Ismay; *Freelove*, John Brown; *Hercules*, Jeremiah Boyes; *Perseverence*, J Carling; *Speedwell*, John Steward; *Delight*, Matthew Smith, and *Providence and Nancy*, Francis Banks jnr[57]. Most of the masters and the ships had been whaling before; in the early years of the war there had been a friendly stand-off between the British and the American whalers, they realised that now France had entered the war things would be getting very much more unpleasant. They were resolved *to take, sink or burn any enemy that should oppose them*. It was reported in the *London Chronicle* that this fleet *is supposed to be the best fitted out for the whale fishery of any in England*. As the ships sailed out of Whitby harbour with their flags flying proudly in the freshening wind, the waving figures on the shore must have felt not only uneasy apprehension but a pride to be part of so noble an enterprise.

A brief moment of cheering patriotism may boost the morale of seamen and of the inhabitants of Whitby; but would not by itself be enough. The ship-owners of vessels about to sail would sit over their hot coffee anxiously scanning the newspapers in the Whitby Coffee House as the bitter February wind howled outside whipping the waves over the harbour walls in a frenzy of foam. Sometimes the news was good: on 20 February news came that a Whitby brig captured by a privateer had been re-captured near Bridlington by the armed ship *Beaver's Prize* and the crew of six who were taking it back to France had been taken prisoner and sent to Hull. Sometimes the news was not so good: the two French privateers that had been haunting the coast between Whitby and Flamborough Head had been seen among a fleet of colliers - scattering them like a fox in a hencoop and capturing many. On 1 March it was reported in the *Public Advertiser* that between them these privateers had taken nearly 50 ships over the previous month. This was likely to be

---

[57] Whitby also sent 5 ships to Greenland. As was customary the Greenland ships, which did not have so far to travel, left later and –if they were lucky- returned sooner than those going to the Davis Straits. They were: *Adamant*, Carlill; *Henrietta*, Bean; *Volunteer*, Coulson; *James and Mary*, Hodgson, and *Loyal Club*, Lattimoor.

something of an exaggeration, but reflected the tenor of the rumours flying wildly among the sailors on the wharves of the Yorkshire ports.

The question in the minds of sailors, owners and merchants was why the valuable trade on the north-east coast had *so long been left a Prey to the Enemy, when it might be effectually prevented by two or three twenty Gun Ships?* The *Newcastle Chronicle* added its voice complaining that a French privateer had spent some time loitering with impunity off the coast just out of range of the cannons at Shields, the article continued *There are three Government Ships lying in the Harbour of Shields; one of which has not stirred these nine Months past. The Government has not, since the commencement of Hostilities with America or France, given any Convoy or Protection to the Trade of this and Ports adjacent, leaving every one to protect himself.*

Captured ships would have their cargo stolen; however, even if there was spare capacity in the privateer's hold it was not worth the time and effort to take on board bulk cargoes like coal and timber which were the mainstay of the North Sea coast trade, so Whitby ships were likely just to have any portable valuables taken. If the vessel itself was worth stealing they would put on her a small crew who would sail her to France or a neutral port: the disadvantage of this was that, with such a small crew, as we have seen, there was the danger of their prize being recaptured. A more practical and profitable course of action was ransoming: hostages (known as *ransomers*) would be taken (usually the master and some apprentices) while the mate and the rest of the crew were allowed home to get the money from the owners. *Jenny*, Petrie, with goods for London, and *Brighthelmstone*, Bennet, carrying coal, both sailing from Shields to London in May 1779 were taken by enemy ships and ransomed for 1,500 and 300 guineas respectively. No wonder ship-owners and merchants were worried.

It was against this background of fear and uncertainty that *General Carleton* set out from Hull on 28 March 1779. It is clear she had been waiting there for some time previously as the mate, cook, carpenter and servants are recorded in the muster roll as being employed from 11 March; Thomas Pyman started on the 14th and the seamen four days later. There was probably a Baltic voyage in March/April that we have no record of, and she most likely sailed with the convoy which left Hull at the beginning of May under the protection of the frigate *Diana*. *General Carleton* then went to Narva returning to Hull on 13 June where she unloaded a cargo of deals and battens for Ralph Dodsworth. There would have been a turn round for new cargoes to be loaded and the appropriate paperwork to be filled in. During that time the depressing news that Spain had joined the war would have reached Hull. A new convoy was collected, and time passed as they waited for the accompanying naval vessel to arrive; it would have been late July or early August before *General Carleton* sailed out of the Humber estuary as part of the Baltic Fleet.

While the ships sailed across the North Sea, the news on the home front was bad, and the panic was palpable; not only had Spain now entered the War, there was even a scare that the French were planning to land on the Isle of Man. The raiding along the north-east coast was frequent, but was not always successful: a Whitby alum ship was chased by an enemy ship which fired at her constantly, doing considerable damage to her keel and rigging, but she managed to outsail her pursuer and reach the safety of Shields. A Scarborough brig was similarly attacked but defended herself, though heavily out gunned; the master was about to strike (lower the flag as a sign of surrender) but his wife who was on board insisted that they should fire a few more shots at their oppressor before giving up - this delay saved the ship as in the extra time they were rescued by the frigate *Jason* sailing south with the Scottish convoy. The narrow escapes only helped highlight the ever-present dangers merchant ships faced, and the seeming shortage of aid: when five vessels were captured off Shields the armed merchant ship *Queen* managed to re-take two of them, while the armed ship *Content*, under hire to the Government, remained in Shields harbour waiting refitting before going to sea. This created a lot of anger in the town.

The complaints about *Content* seem finally to have hit home, and the Government took action as on 15 August we find her, armed with 20 guns, defending *Freelove*, John Brown, with 14 guns. The Whitby whaler was being threatened by two French privateers, armed with 24 and 18 six-pounders respectively which were at first flying English flags, off the island of Cocket.[58] According to *Lloyds' Evening Post*, *Freelove* fired about 160 and *Content* around 400 shot, the privateers evading capture with judicious flight. An officer on board *Content* described the action thus: *We engaged them near four Glasses, with Grape Shot flying like Showers of Hail; shot away their Colours twice, raked them for and aft, and made their sides like a Riddle. Content's* sails and rigging were much damaged, and they had one man killed and two wounded. The officer added that *If the Greenlandman had supported us, we should have probably brought them both into Shields...but being a Merchant Ship she made towards the Shore, imagining we should be taken.* Whatever the truth of the matter the varying accounts reflect a deal of mutual suspicion and mistrust between the Royal Navy and the merchant marine. After the engagement *Content* met other whalers which she guided into Whitby harbour.

In addition to the dangers of enemy ships, the natural hazards of the North Sea coast continued to take their toll as well: the brig *Nelly* of Newcastle with a cargo of kelp bound for the alum works at Whitby in the autumn of 1779 was wrecked on the Orkneys after having all her sails ripped away in a violent gale. All the crew, except the carpenter, were drowned as were two young female passengers.

John Paul Jones continued regularly raiding round the coast; now that France was in the war he was better equipped. He commanded a squadron, his own ship being *Bonhomme Richard* with a crew of 380 and 40 guns. His activities were widely reported, and he came to haunt the imaginations of those that lived on the coast, and there was an expectation that Jones intended to make a landing on the Yorkshire coast. It is said that his name was invoked to scare young children to behave, but certainly there was fear of this demonised American who *came out of the Sea* to attack, despoil and plunder. Robert Holt describes how, *whenever Paul Jones...was reported to be in the neighbourhood, wagons were kept packed with valuables and ladies held themselves ready to start inland at a moment's notice.* Such was his reputation that some captures were probably attributed to him that were actually made by other predatory captains. The newspapers then as now were not always accurate in their reporting: for example the account in 1779 of the total wreck of the Whitby ship *Endeavour*, Jackson, with the loss of all hands was rather premature as she survived until 1809. There was even a report, mentioned by Bagshawe, that Jones had sailed with impunity into Whitby harbour *while the people were in church*; this not only underestimates the vigilance and effectiveness of the batteries but also overestimates the proportion of the population who went to church. It is also difficult to imagine Jones not exploiting such a situation by doing a bit of pillaging and burning. Gaskin tells the tale that Paul Jones passed close enough to Whitby to be in range of her battery which fired, but *their cannon burst and two gunners were blown over the cliff and killed.* He is confusing the events of 1779 with an event in 1782 when Robert Johnson *was killed by firing E Battery Gunns*, and the 22-year-old soldier John Peak *was unfortunately killed at the same time.* They were both buried in

---

[58] Coquet Island is off the Northumberland coast, near Warkworth. It is now an RSPB reserve.

the churchyard at Whitby, not far from where they died, on 22 February, and the details quoted here come from the burial register. Such was the enduring power of John Paul Jones to attract legendary stories.

The Baltic convoy of 41 merchant ships, of which *General Carleton* was very likely one, under the protection of the frigate *Serapis*, captain Pearson, 44 guns, and the armed ship *Countess of Scarborough*, captain Piercy, 20 guns, was returning south to Hull. They had passed Filey at about 2pm on 23 September when they saw a group of ships rounding Flamborough Head flying British colours, but nonetheless looking very like privateers. It was in fact John Paul Jones' *Bonhomme Richard* and the rest of his vessels: the frigate *Alliance*, 36 guns, *Pallas*, 32 guns, and *Vengeance*, 12 guns. Pearson, immediately sensing danger, attempted to bring his two fighting ships between Jones' squadron and the convoy allowing them to head for friendly ports, while Jones tried to avoid him doing so. This rather complex manoeuvring and counter-manoeuvring took most of the afternoon. Once Jones realised that he was not going to be able to plunder the merchant vessels with impunity he ordered his ships to form a line of battle, and Pearson's gunners were called to arms. As *Bonhomme Richard* was still flying the British flag, Pearson asked what ship she was, the answer was *Princess Royal*, to which the response was *Where from?* Receiving no reply, Pearson demanded they identify themselves properly or he would be *under the necessity of firing*. Jones struck the British colours, raising the stars and stripes and ordering his crew to fire at *Serapis*. This was about seven o'clock and night had fallen.

Although Jones had ordered a line of battle, that was not what happened. *Alliance*, captained by a Frenchman who seemed neither to respect nor to obey Jones, spent much of the time dithering, and *Vengeance* similarly seems to have been fairly useless. Had there been a line of battle Jones would theoretically have outgunned his opponents, but he found himself alone facing *Serapis* which was more heavily armed, an imbalance that was exacerbated when two of Jones' guns exploded during his second broadside killing several of his men and causing damage to other guns and to the ship itself. Jones realised that his only hope was to get in close to *Serapis* which he did, grappling the ships together. *Countess of Scarborough* realised that it could not effectively continue to attack *Bonhomme Richard* without the possibility of hitting *Serapis*, and attacked *Pallas;* these two ships were then some distance away, so the battle turned into two separate duels. At eight o'clock the moon rose: bright, clear and full enabling the whole battle to be seen from the shore by an ever-increasing crowd of spectators.

There ensued a furiously fought duel between *Bonhomme Richard* and *Serapis*, the latter pounding the sides of Jones' ship at point blank with its heavy guns, and the former responding with tenacious ferocity with everything it could muster in one of the fiercest two-ship engagements in the age of sail. At one point there was a rumour on *Bonhomme Richard* that she was sinking and that Jones was dead; and Pearson, close enough to hear their discussions, demanded, *Do you ask for quarter?* To which Jones, very much alive, responded in French which can be translated as: *That hadn't occurred to me; I am determined to make you ask **me** for quarter*[59].

After a two-hour battle *Countess of Scarborough* surrendered to *Pallas*. *Alliance*, which had been on the periphery of this action then spent some time in debate with *Pallas* about which ship would take possession of the prize; eventually she sailed over to try and

---

[59] In a romanticised account from the 1820s this was rendered (rather too freely) as *I have not yet begun to fight*, which is the phrase that has since become inseparable from the John Paul Jones legend.

Fig 10: The Battle of Flamborough Head.

help *Bonhomme Richard*, though she seems to have inflicted more friendly fire than actual aid, before withdrawing to a safe distance.

At 10.30 after two and a half hours of close-quarter fighting, a grenade thrown from one of the yards of *Bonhomme Richard* exploded on the deck of *Serapis* doing considerable damage, and it looked as if the mast would fall. Captain Pearson realised there was little benefit in prolonging the action any further and surrendered.

It was *a famous victory* though something of a Pyrrhic one. The entire convoy of merchant ships had sailed into port unharmed, most into Scarborough. *Bonhomme Richard* was reduced to little more than a floating colander, and despite valiant efforts to save her she sank the following morning[60] About half of Jones' crew were killed or wounded; *Serapis* had suffered slightly fewer casualties; *Alliance* had suffered none. John Paul Jones now took *Serapis* as his flagship, and with *Alliance, Pallas, Vengeance* and the captured *Countess of Scarborough* sailed to Holland.

The story ran and ran in the newspapers. Several men who claimed to have been captured by Jones and later escaped gave their own accounts, one asserting that during the engagement *Jones stood on the quarter-deck with a brace of pistols, and shot three of his own men.* These accounts may well contain some truth, or at least no less truth than Jones' own account which he wrote in 1785 when the American government had tired of him and

---

[60] A wreck has been found which may be that of *Bonhomme Richard*.

31: The *Endeavour* replica at London. This gives a good idea of what *General Carleton*, and *Valiant*, would have looked like from the side view. After returning from Cook's first voyage, *Endeavour* was sold. After a change of name she reappeared as *Lord Sandwich*, and she was one of the transports ships which was sunk at Newport in 1778.

he was looking for a job. He hoped, unsuccessfully as it turned out, to get a command in the French navy.

An interesting, and probably quite accurate account was given by an inhabitant of Scarborough on 26 September and appeared in the *London Chronicle*: *On Wednesday the red flag was hoisted out at the castle, as a signal that an enemy was on the coast, which was Paul Jones and his fleet. He had been about here several days, which put the inhabitants and strangers into a fright, insomuch that several left the town. Soon after our arrival on Thursday evening, we were told there was an engagement at sea; I immediately threw up the sash of the room I was in, and we had a fair view of the engagement, which appeared very severe, for the firing was frequently so quick, that we could scarce count the shots...All the town was in alarm; the Cumberland Militia, which is quartered here, beat to arms, and have been on duty both night and day ever since.*

General Carleton eventually arrived safely in Hull, and all the crew were signed off for the winter on October 14.

Even in winter, when most vessels were laid up for a few months, the dangers did not stop. The Whitby armed ship *Jane* single-handed managed to chase off two French privateers in December though she was so damaged that she *arrived off Whitby in a shattered Condition*. However there was a good reason for most ships to avoid the North Sea coast in winter as the three French privateers that sailed from Boulogne on 8 December were to discover. They were overwhelmed by a heavy gale in which they were separated, and one of them, the 10-gun *Bellona*, was not only severely battered but lost 30 sailors washed overboard in the tempest. The wrecked vessel was driven ashore near Whitby, with only six bedraggled men aboard who no doubt regretted their rash and avaricious enterprise.

Chapter 8

1780
The Press Gang

Sailors feared many things: being blown onto a lee shore, a fire at sea, being captured by the enemy, growing old in poverty, John Paul Jones; but perhaps what they feared most was impressment into the Navy.

This is not to say that there were not plenty of young men who, as James Cook did, signed up voluntarily to serve in the Royal Navy, made a good career of it and did not dislike it; but of the several autobiographies by sailors of the Georgian Era a common theme is the constant vigilance not to fall into the hands of the press gang. Even John Nicol, who *longed to be at sea*, wanted to sail in merchant ships. He was eventually impressed into the Navy and after a long service returned to his beloved Scotland. When war was again declared *the press-gang came in quest* of him. His wife was frantic at the prospect of losing him and gave him no peace until he had sold his stock in trade and most of his furniture and moved inland away from the clutches of the press. He described life in the Navy as *a bondage that had been imposed upon me against my will, and no hopes or relief until the end of the war.* Landsman Hay had run away to sea as a boy to gain a post on a merchantman but was impressed twice and escaped twice. When asked why he did not want to volunteer he replied, *I get much better wages in the merchant service and should I be unable to agree with the Captain I am at liberty to leave him at the end of the voyage.* William Robinson,[61] in his memoirs, states that *the many cruel and heart-rending cases of impressments which I have witnessed both at sea and in harbour, are too many to stow away in this work.* One sailor, having been pressed, hanged himself.

The pressing of men into the Navy struck at the roots of the deeply held British belief in individual freedom, and was always unpopular, an article in *The Gentlemen's Magazine* of 1741 describing it as *the Slavery of those who most contribute to Freedom.* Until being a sailor in the Navy became a real career option for the men, rather than just for the officers, there was little incentive to give up working on merchantmen. Recruitment officers spoke enticingly of the spoils of prize ships captured, but in reality seamen had too small a share to make a significant difference. Various bounties were offered to persuade sailors to volunteer in the hopes of reducing the necessity for impressments, for example in May 1778 the *principal Gentlemen* of Whitby were offering £5 (£35,600) to any able seaman, and half that amount for an ordinary seaman, who agreed to enlist in the Navy and sail on the armed tender *Charming Betsey* that was recruiting in the town at that time.

However, with the size of the Royal Navy rapidly expanding and shrinking as war and peace demanded, impressments had become an essential part of the necessary system of manning the ships of war. Contrary to the popular image of a press-gang sweeping through a town and taking anyone whom they happened to find on the streets or in the ale-houses, in the period in question nearly all the men taken were seamen or shipyard workers, and a

---

[61] He wrote under the pseudonym *Jack Nastyface*, presumably his nickname, just as the sailor John Cremer, who wrote his memoirs, was called *Ramblin' Jack*. It can be assumed that the majority of sailors would have acquired such nicknames.

considerable proportion of sailors were seized: Ralph Davis suggests that three quarters of the country's merchant seamen were taken into the Navy during the Seven Years War. In 1775 the Navy had just under 20,000 men; this had risen to more than 30,000 by the following year, rising by about 20,000 per year to 1778, and by 1780 was just short of 100,000. This dramatic rise was the result of a number of factors, but primarily due to impressments. In 1780 the Navy Office commissioned a report on the Impress Service covering the previous year; it reported that in total the service employed 1,019 personnel on shore who, between 1 Jan and 31 Dec 1779, raised a total of 21,367 men for the Navy at a cost of £106,591-5-1 (£130 million, or about £6,000 per man). In the same period 4,544 men had been *discharged unserviceable* from the Navy.

Although it was often believed at the time, as it is sometimes now, that the practice was illegal, this was not the case. At best a very ethically dubious pursuit, the press employed all kinds of unpleasantness and subterfuge to achieve its ends: the 1780 accounts not only list money paid to *Constables and others for apprehending stragling seamen*, but also *Rewards to informers for discovering secreted seamen*. Impressment was not only much feared and much evaded, but also much resisted: there are several instances of seamen not only coming to blows with impress men, but also of shots being fired and men wounded or even killed. Small wonder then that another section in the accounts was for *Law Charges…in defending Officers and others employed in Raising Men*.

There were basically two ways the press used to catch their victims: landing in a port and making a surprise roundup of seamen, or intercepting ships returning to port and taking men off them. Whitby was a good target for the first method with possibly some 3,000 sailors and a considerable number of shipyard workers together making up a sizeable proportion of its male population. For the press, timing was everything, in winter when most of the sailors were ashore, they could be difficult to find. The best time would be in the Spring when the sailing season began and sailors were thronging the quayside eager to find work aboard ship. Even so it was amazing how quickly sailors could 'disappear' once the navy tender was seen approaching the harbour. In 1780 the events of 1753 would still be a living memory to many, to others a warning tale told by their parents: in early March of that year a tender put in to Whitby harbour, with her yards lowered and hidden, pretending to have been damaged in a gale and needing repairs before sailing north. They maintained the deceit by buying new yards from a local raff merchant and making much show of looking as if they were busy attending to the rigging. Once they were sure they had allayed suspicion and under cover of darkness they *carried off all the able Seamen then on board the Vessels lying* in the harbour *being upwards of 100, and securing them on board, weighed Anchor next Tide, and put to Sea with a fair wind.*

But the depredations of Whitby by the press were not just a matter of history. The Whitby whaler *Adamant* was particularly successful in 1779, leaving the ice of the Greenland sea on 18 June having caught eight whales which would ensure not only a good profit for the owners, but also bonuses for all the crew. As the ship sailed homewards down the coast a cheer must have gone up when the crew first spotted the distinctive outline of Whitby, with the squat parish church perched atop East Cliff, promising the joys of being reunited with family and loved ones, of basking lazily in the warm sunshine and of home cooking. As *Adamant* arrived in Whitby Road, she was intercepted by his majesty's sloop *Fury* and the armed tender *Advice* which *boarded her and impressed all her hands.* As the sailor Edward Barlow wrote, *It is a very bad thing for a poor seaman when he is pressed in this manner, for if he have a wife and children he in not suffered to go to see them.*

94

The part *Freelove* played in fighting the French privateers in August of 1779 is debatable: maybe she fired 160 shots at the enemy or *made towards the Shore*, or both. But one thing is certain: it was no accident that the government armed ship *Content* was nearby, as she had just impressed a dozen of the whaler's crew.

And when after the privateers had been chased away *Content* joined another five ships of the fleet returning from the Davis Straits, and convoyed them home to Whitby, it was about as friendly an act as a wolf convoying a herd of sheep. It was a humiliating return for a fleet that had set out with such bravado, not only were men impressed from each of the vessels, but the whaling had not been very successful either. Tony Barrow records that over the next two years, the Whitby whaling fleet halved in size.

Sailors were also vulnerable when employed by the Navy Board on transports. It was common for ships of the Royal Navy, who lost men through disease, desertion and battle to impress seamen from transports which were conveniently to hand. However the charter parties[62] which laid down the terms of the hiring of transports specified a strict minimum number of seamen based on the ship's tonnage (though the number was reduced over time). Masters of transports would often find themselves unable to sail as they were without sufficient mariners to man their ship according to the charter party after they had lost members of the crew pressed into the Navy. This is exactly what happened to the Whitby ship *Elizabeth*, John Pressick master, Christopher Pressick owner, as explained in the 1779-80 muster roll. For a month she was detained idle in London on *Account of the Impress*; left with a non-viable crew of *only Eight Men & Boyes* who had to be discharged while more men could be found to make up the full complement once more. This was clearly very inefficient; the Admiralty, the Navy Board and the Army all were autonomous organisations theoretically serving a common end, but often competing with each other. Lord Howe had made it quite clear how crucial transports were when he wrote in 1778 that *the subsistence of the army immediately and entirely depends upon them*.

Apart from ships in the whaling trade, or at the start or end of the sailing season, there were not many vessels entering or leaving Whitby, so it was not so profitable for Navy impressment tenders to lurk outside it; Hull would be a much better target. It has been mentioned before that it was possible that Pyman took *General Carleton* into Whitby before taking her cargo into Hull. Another reason for doing this would be to foil the press. In Whitby he could discharge the seamen, and then take the ship to Hull manned only by the master, mate, carpenter and the apprentices who were normally exempt from impressments, so if the ship was stopped the crew (in theory at least) were safe. While in Whitby he would have made an agreement with sailors for the next season. It was not unusual for a master to connive with the seamen on board to enable them to evade impressments.

When *General Carleton* sailed from Hull on 24 March 1780 Thomas Pyman was master of a rather strangely-composed crew. Thomas Williamson was still mate, William Taylor the carpenter, and James Watson the cook. John Corner, seaman on the ship for the previous three years was now 2nd mate. There were four seamen: James Derry who had sailed on *General Carleton* twice before, Robert Deighton, James Nixon and James Forbes. But whereas in 1777 there had been seven apprentices, forming less than 40% of the crew; now there were 13 apprentices comprising some 60% of the crew. Zacharias Campion (though only 13) had left, so had George Stockton who, at 18, had probably completed his

---

[62] This was the contract between the Navy Board and the owner, or agent, who was hiring out the vessel. It was called *party*, as each party to the agreement had a copy.

apprenticeship. George Littlefair returned after a year's absence, and John Johnson was away for a year. William Johnson, possibly his brother, was new, as was Cornelius Cayley.

The disproportionately large number of servants may reflect the shortage of seamen after the press had taken so many to join the Navy, or the fact that apprentices were cheap; or it may be that apprentices, provided they were under eighteen or in the first three years of apprenticeship, had protection from impressments. This involved them applying for a certificate and providing proof of identity and status as an apprentice. The document was addressed to *all Commanders of His Majesty's Ships Press masters, and others whom it doth or may concern* who were instructed *not to Impress him into His Majesty's Service.* The document would be dated and have a number of signatures. Because there was a flourishing trade in misappropriating such exemptions they included not just the servant's name but also description. Anyone found in possession of such a document that was not issued for him would be instantly pressed.

Fragments of such a document were found among the artefacts raised from the wreck of *General Carleton*. It had been placed inside a flat, rectangular tin box with rounded edges and no lid.

Fig 11: Drawing of the tin alloy container into which the exemption of press document had been carefully folded.

Unfortunately only parts of the printed words of the *pro forma* have survived, the name and description have not. It is remarkable that readable fragments of paper had endured underwater, covered in its protective tar, for over 200 years, and pleasing that it was identifiable. As the war was over in 1785, this document is most likely to have belonged to an apprentice who had joined *General Carleton* before peace was declared in 1783 though impressments (albeit on a much smaller scale) did continue in peacetime. However the likelihood is that it belonged to a younger apprentice rather than one in their final year, so I suspect that the owner was probably James Hart, John Noble or John Thompson.

It was possible for a ship to obtain an exemption from press if it was deemed to be engaged in vital work; in the *Three Sisters'* accounts there is a record of a payment for 15 shillings (£75; £825) *To a Protection.* The official record of such protections in the National Archives is patchy and does not cover the *General Carleton* years, but exemptions were

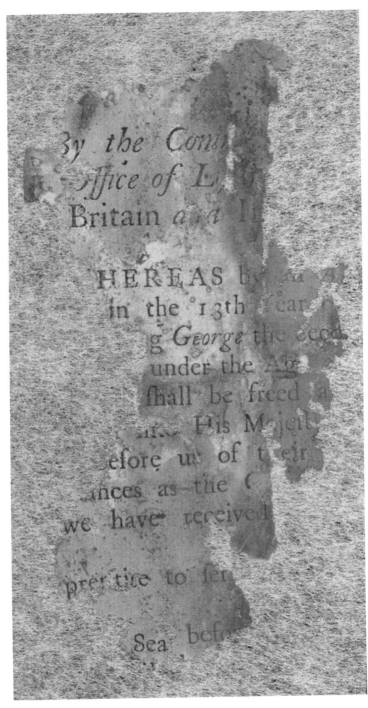

32: A fragment of the exemption from press document, probably issued to James Hart, John Noble or John Thompson.

given to many ships in the Norway and Baltic trade, so it is possible that Pyman had such an exemption for the ship when she sailed from Hull to the White Sea port of Onega in ballast returning with a cargo of timber. Just such a document was issued on 5 October 1787 (in peacetime) to Thomas Pyman for *Peggy*, destination the Baltic with 18 men.

It was probably as she approached Hull that *General Carleton* was stopped by one of His Majesty's armed tenders on 25 May, and a naval officer came on board with a posse of sailors. The apprentices would have fetched their documentation to show that they had exemption. The officer's attention then turned to the seamen, and James Nixon was duly impressed into the Navy. We have no details except the muster roll's terse comment *Imprest at Sea*. If the ship had a protection from press it had been ignored, a not unusual occurrence.

The muster roll records that the crew were all finally paid off at Hull on 15 November 1780. So far as is known it was the last time that *General Carleton* entered that port.

Chapter 9

1780 - 1781
Working for the Government

1780 started on a gloomy note in Whitby as news arrived of the sinking of *Prince of Wales* with all hands on 1 December 1779. The loss of a ship is bad news, but the loss of an entire crew is a tragedy. The master, George Pressick, though from South Shields, would have been known and respected by many in Whitby. Aware of the fate of the man and the ship, it is poignant to read what du Roi wrote of the 1776 voyage: *He* [George Pressick[63] who would have been 44 at the time] *had given up seafaring, was a man of means and married, and living happily with his family. He had undertaken this journey, against the wishes of his wife, out of gratitude to an old friend, because no one else could be found who would undertake the trip on such an old dilapidated ship as ours.*

The old friend would presumably have been John Holt, Nathaniel Campion's father-in-law who had owned *Prince of Wales*[64] for over 30 years. The *dilapidated old ship* had been in the service as a transport since 1776 when it would have been subjected to a Navy Board inspection. This was quite rigorous – for example, *Lord Sandwich* (ex-*Endeavour*) failed her first inspection and had to have repairs done before re-submitting, being finally accepted in February 1776. *Prince of Wales* had undergone lengthening and total repairs in 1771, but there is no record of anything serious since then. It is not known what caused her to sink – presumably it was an Atlantic storm.

The family with whom George Pressick had been living so happily, and whom he had possibly not seen since 1776, included his wife Mary (née Carling of Stokesley) and his children: George and Barbara, who would have been 7 and 3 when he left them, and Ann who was born on 18 August 1776, some months after he had sailed. In addition to George Pressick, the muster roll recording the loss of *Prince of Wales* lists as *Drowned* the carpenter William Pinkney, Blackburn Carling and 22 *seamen names unknown*.

William Pinkney, also from Shields, had been a servant on Adam Boulby's ship *Dorothy and Esther* in 1768 when Thomas Pyman was master. He left two children: Margaret aged 4 and Ann aged 2. They, like George Pressick's children, received support from the Whitby Seaman's Fund, as did Ann, the widow of Blackburn Carling.

Blackburn Carling (or Carlin, Carlill or Carlisle) could possibly have been a relative of George Pressick's wife. He was certainly known to the Holts and to *Prince of Wales* on which he had previously sailed between 1757 and 1759 when it had been a transport taking troops to America during the Seven Years' War. He had also been on the crew of *Olive Branch* (1753-1755) and *Royal Briton* (1777-1779) – two other vessels owned by the Holt family. On all these occasions he was employed as a carpenter. He had left *Royal Briton* on

---

[63] The earliest record of George was of him serving as a 16-year-old servant on *Lawrell* [Laurel]. The master was the 31-year-old Christopher Pressick, the owner William Barker.

[64] It is possible she was the *Prince of Wales* transport ship which had served as a prison ship in Wallabout Bay New York, alongside *Whitby*. Prison ships were usually older and less seaworthy vessels, which would fit. But that ship allegedly did not commence being a prison ship until 1779 and was burnt at New York, so it is unlikely.

27 September 1779 at New York and almost immediately had joined *Prince of Wales*. It is likely that he was transferred to the latter ship as an act of charity because she was going home to Britain and he was getting old. Pressick may well have welcomed the thought of having a second carpenter on his dilapidated ship. In the event Carling had only been part of the crew for a month before the disaster.

There are Navy Board musters for *Prince of Wales* while in America. They can give some insight into who the 22 unnamed seamen were who also drowned that December day. For example, it seems highly probable that Miles Rogan was the cook who lost *his favourite dog* in the storm on 17 April 1776, and who drowned when the ship went down.

This sombre mood over lost friends would have found an echo on Friday February 4 1780. As Parson Woodforde records in his Diary, this was a day *for a General Fast to be observed thro' the Kingdom, to beg almighty God his assistance in our present troubles being at open rupture with America, France and Spain, and a blessing on our Fleets and Armies; I therefore went to...Church...and read the proper Prayers on the Occasion.* This would have been done in all churches up and down the country, including Whitby where at St Mary's Parish Church and at the newly erected chapel at Baxtergate the surrogate vicar Richard Robertson or the curate Henry Archer would have led the congregation in the prescribed prayers:

O Almighty God, King of all kings, and Governour of all things, whose power no creature is able to resist, to whom it belongeth justly to punish sinners, and to be merciful to them that truly repent; Save and deliver us, we humbly beseech thee, from the hands of our enemies; abate their pride, assuage their malice, and confound their devices, that we, being armed with thy defence, may be preserved evermore from all perils, to glorifie thee, who art the only giver of all victory, through the merits of thy only Son Jesus Christ our Lord.

- The words receiving perhaps a more heartfelt *Amen* than usual.

Whether the crews of the ships leaving Whitby harbour that spring felt particularly blessed, or whether James Nixon saw his impressment as God working in his mysterious way to enhance the capability of the British Royal Navy is not recorded. However what is certain is that at about this time Nathaniel Campion, with the agreement of the other owners, decided that *General Carleton* should follow his other two ships *Thomas & Richard* and *Valiant* into Government service.

Thomas and Richard had continued to be a transport. We know that on 22 May 1776 she carried members of the 29th Regiment, fresh from their success in relieving the siege of Quebec, upstream to Three Rivers. She then apparently went to the West Indies, being recorded as arriving at Deal from St Vincent in August 1777. Between April and June of 1778 she was transporting soldiers of the 10th Regiment from Greenock to Portsmouth. This is presumably Portsmouth in Virginia, at the mouth of Chesapeke Bay, as it takes her more that two months to get there from the Clyde. While she is at Portsmouth she receives on board 12 men of the 21st Regiment from the Whitby transport *William and Mary*, John Knaggs, which had also sailed from Greenock. After that the history of *Thomas and Richard* becomes obscure; there is a *Thomas and Richard* of Whitby which becomes a privateer in 1778 which may be the same vessel. Cuthbert Park, who had been her captain from at least 1774 became master of the newly-built 350-ton ship *Otterington*, owned by Margaret Campion's brother William, in 1781, which may suggest that *Thomas and Richard* was lost by then; she certainly did not survive until compulsory registration in 1786. She was an old vessel, probably built in 1749, and Nathaniel Campion would have known her for nearly all her life and most of his own, first when his brother John (*Jacky*) was master, then when he took command of her after his brother drowned, and finally as managing owner.

The Whitby coffee house would have subscribed to a number of journals, and the *London Gazette*, would certainly have been one. It was then, as it is now, *the official newspaper of record in the United Kingdom*. The shipowners would read it regularly, not just to see who has gone bankrupt, but to look out for government offers to tender for contracts. These would be similar to this one, from 1775:

Navy Office March 6 1775
The Principal Officers and Commissioners of His Majesty's Navy give Notice, that they will be ready to treat with such Persons as are willing to contract for the Stores under-mentioned, for His Majesty's Service, on the Day against the same expressed, at Twelve o'Clock at Noon, that they may attend with Proposals accordingly

Norway Goods	*Tuesday 28 March*
Foreign Plank and Prussia Deals	*Friday March 31*
East Country Tar	*Tuesday April 4*
Hemp	*Friday April 7*
Iron	*Tuesday April 11*

These were exactly the sort of goods which *Thomas and Richard* and *Valiant* had been transporting for private merchants for many years; and from the time that Thomas Pyman had become master of *Valiant* in 1773 she had been providing them for the Government. Between 1776 and 1779 Richard Thompson had been master of *Valiant*, during which time she seems to have been commuting between Cork, one of the main victualling centres, and London.

With the loss of *Thomas & Richard*, Nathaniel Campion clearly thought that *Valiant* should replace her as a transport ship, and *General Carleton* should in turn replace *Valiant*, working for the government on this side of the Atlantic.

This involved *Valiant* having a new master, and the man who was chosen was William Hustler. He was experienced in the transport business, as he had commanded Henry Clarke's ship *Saville* since 1775. Campion submitted *Valiant* for a transport, it was measured as 341.44 tons, accepted as suitable and was *ready to enter into pay* on 8 February 1780. The agent Alex Curling recording the mustering of the *Valiant* and her crew on 19 Nov 1780 and 16 March, 1 May and 9 June 1781.

In 1780 *General Carleton* started working on government contract. On 14 June she arrived at Portsmouth from Riga, leaving -bound for Riga once more- on 6 July. The clear inference is that she was supplying the Naval Dockyards at Portsmouth. Riga exported a range of timber, but was also famous for masts.

It was in midsummer 1780 that the shipowners scanning the papers in the Whitby coffee house read some information that made it seem as if the prayers of the British had indeed been answered: on 12 May General Clinton had captured Charlestown.

This was part of a new war strategy by the British Government. It was based on the enduring belief which had prompted the disastrous North Carolina campaign of 1776, namely that in the South there were large numbers of Loyalists who, with encouragement and support from the British Army, would rise up and take power. The plan was to set up firm bases with deep water harbours where army and navy could protect each other if threatened and from which campaigns could be put into operation to reclaim the south, which was considered to be an achievable goal. At the same time a strong presence would be established in Virginia to drive a wedge between the rebellious northern states and the wealthy southern states which were funding them, hoping that the former would then not have the money to continue the war.

One of the Whitby ships engaged in the ambitious amphibious operation to capture Charlestown was *Royal Briton* which had been based at New York as a transport since 1777. It was no doubt to avoid taking him into this battle that Blackburn Carling had been sent home on *Prince of Wales*. William Sleightholm who had been master of *Royal Briton* for over two years was discharged at New York in November 1779 and the mate Roger Galilee became captain. It was on 26 December that Clinton set out from New York with 30 ships of war and 8,700 soldiers in 88 transports among which there would have been several Whitby vessels, *Royal Briton* being one. The progress of this fleet was hampered by appalling winds, with many of the transports becoming scattered. The main body of ships arrived in late January but the rest of the surviving vessels struggled in over the next six or seven weeks, often in a very poor state. Several transports that were delayed had run out of food, the ship that was carrying the artillery had sunk, and most of the horses had been thrown overboard to save the ship or because there was no fodder for them. *Royal Briton* survived. It was a bad start to a brilliant campaign, and was the most successful action of the war with some 5,000 American soldiers taken prisoner.

As events were to reveal, the belief in the vast mass of southern Loyalists was a myth. There were some, of course, including Thomas Brown son of Jonas Brown of Whitby. Jonas Brown was a master-mariner living in Grape Lane in 1743, next door to the master mariners William Skinner on one side and Thomas Hunter on the other, and in the same short street as Mrs Esther Walker, the sailmaker James Atty, and the master mariners Abel Chapman and Benjamin Lotherington. In 1764 Jonas Brown's daughter Jane married Jonathan Lacy[65]; their marriage was witnessed by Samuel Pressick and Jane's sister Mary who, in 1777, married Edward Cayley. Edward's son Cornelius, by his first wife, sailed on *General Carleton*.

Jonas Brown, later shipowner and gentleman, financed his son Thomas in a money-making settlement venture. Thomas would sail to Georgia with emigrants he recruited locally and from Scotland and the Orkneys, and he would receive grants of land in the *newly ceded valuable lands* in Georgia: 200 acres for the head of a family and a further 50 for each member of his family. Male settlers would be allowed to occupy 15 acres (with additional land for a wife and for children) of Brown's land rent-free for five years, and be given a house and sufficient stock, seeds and equipment to set themselves up. This would be leave plenty of land in Brown's occupation as a plantation for him to settle as a country gentleman, and once the rents started coming in he would be very prosperous.

They sailed on Jonas' ship *Marlborough*, with George Pressick (later master of *Prince of Wales*) as captain, in 1774 from Whitby to Savannah. Thomas Brown duly received 5,600 acres, and set about building up Brownsborough, his new plantation. He had soon realised the anti-British agitation was not confined to the area round Boston, as had been the opinion in England when he left. He remained loyal to the British establishment, became a magistrate and refused to recognise the newly formed Georgian Provincial Congress. Edward Cashin, who tells Brown's story in his book *The King's Ranger*, records how on 2 August 1775 he was visited by a delegation of about a hundred Liberty Boys who sought to force him to renounce his allegiance to the Crown and to support the revolution.

---

[65] Jonathan was a roper at Spital Bridge. Prosperity enabled him to live at Larpool Hall, and he was briefly a shipbuilder, but became a bankrupt in 1803. His sister Mary married Thomas Lotherington, master mariner, in 1756, and their daughter Mary married William Holt, Margaret Campion's brother.

He refused, was attacked and for a while managed to defend himself with pistols and a sword; but was overpowered and tied to a tree. *His hair was stripped off with knives, he was scalped in three or four places, and his legs were tarred and burned so badly that he lost two toes and could not walk properly for several months.*

On 15 December 1775 *Marlborough* returned to Georgia, this time with Thomas Walker as master, with another shipload of settlers; as before many were small farmers from the north of Scotland dispossessed by what was to become known as the Highland Clearances. Too poor to pay the cost of their voyage, they came as indentured servants. Also on the ship was Isaac Herbert, Thomas Brown's agent, who was possibly the elder brother of William Herbert of Goathland who was master of Nathaniel Campion's *Valiant* between 1764 and 1773.

Exiled from Georgia, Thomas Brown formed a loyalist group, called at first the East Florida Rangers and later the King's Rangers. However, whatever the extent of loyalist sympathy in the southern states, there were few who were prepared to go against the populist mood and risk a visit from the Liberty Boys, let alone take up arms against their fellow countrymen for German King and British Country. The southern campaign was not a success.

1780 was not a good year for the British: in August a combined Spanish and French fleet attacked a British convoy of merchant ships in the West Indies, capturing 55 vessels. This not only damaged trade, but was an enormous blow to prestige and morale. In December war was declared with the Dutch, so the British Army was fighting not only the Americans but also the French, Spanish and Dutch; what had started as a war for American Independence had become an international fight for trade and territory.

In 1781 *General Carleton* continued with much the same crew doing much the same work, the muster roll stating the year's sailing officially began in London on 25 March. James Watson was replaced as cook by Edward Walker. William Daniel had left, otherwise the previous year's servants were all back, though John Featherstone who had finished his apprenticeship was appointed 2nd mate. John Johnson returned, and there was a new apprentice Richard Wrightson. The three seamen were all new: Francis Stephenson, Thomas Stonehouse and William Pattison. Another change was that *General Carleton* was now delivering the cargoes loaded in Riga and Petersburg to London presumably at the shipyard at Deptford.

For Nathaniel Campion the business of ship-owning seemed to be going well. Thomas Pyman was proving to be an excellent master mariner, who had developed his skills and his contacts in the Baltic trade, and whose practical advice was very useful when the owners of *General Carleton* met together to discuss strategy. William Hustler was proving skilful as captain of a transport ship, being able to foster a good spirit among the crew. Profits were looking good, and it was time for expansion. The decision was made, presumably in early 1781 to commission a new vessel, the owners were Nathaniel Campion, his elder brother Samuel, father-in-law John Holt, brother-in-law Thomas Holt, Christopher Richardson who had recently married Nathaniel's sister-in-law Mary Holt and Thomas Pyman. The ship was to be called *Peggy*, and Thomas Pyman was to be the managing owner, presumably owning a more major share than he did for *General Carleton*. He had prospered as a master mariner and part-owner of *General Carleton*, and Adam Boulby who died in March 1780 at the age of 76 had remembered his *former servant* in his will.

Pyman would be master of *Peggy* which would trade with the Baltic ports, something which he knew well, and permitted him to spend time in the winter months with his wife Esther and his children Esther (11) and Thomas (7). According to the muster roll *General*

Carleton arrived at London on 1 December, and all the crew were paid off. Whether the ship overwintered in London, or it was run up to Whitby is open to question. One thing is clear: when Thomas Pyman stepped off the vessel in December 1781 that was the end of his time as her master: the captaincy passed to William Hustler, and *General Carleton* would serve the government in the overseas theatre of war.

Chapter 10

1781 - 1783
The End of the American War

There had been some debate, and dithering, about which would be the best place in Virginia to establish a British base for the campaign to sever the American north from the funds generated in the south. It had to be accessible, defensible, with good communications and able to accommodate warships. Eventually Yorktown, or Little York as it was also called, was chosen and troops were moved there.

In August 1780 General Cornwallis was established in Yorktown with an army of some size though rather battered by recent skirmishes in the unsuccessful campaigns in the south. Yorktown is on a comparatively narrow part of the mouth of York River, and Cornwallis had not only defended the town but also had a stronghold across the river at Gloucester Point. The river flowed into Chesapeake Bay near the estuary mouth between Cape Charles and Cape Henry, so Yorktown was not much over 30 miles from the sea. He had with him a fleet of over 70 vessels mainly transports so he could embark his troops if required, or be supplied by sea.

Among the vessels in Cornwallis' fleet were several vessels with Whitby connections[66]:

The 247-ton ship *Cochran* was built in Whitby in 1770, but was owned by W Cunningham of Glasgow. She was a privateer, mounting 22 guns and with a crew of 80. With Thomas Bolton as master she had cruised the Bay of Biscay *to assail the enemies of Britain*, and is reported in April 1788 to have captured the schooner *Independence*, Pattent, from Baltimore bound for Bordeaux with a cargo of tobacco, and taken her into Glasgow. This was the second prize she had seized in that area. In April 1779 *Cochran* arrived at Antigua, probably as a transport as part of the move to reinforce the British possessions in the Lesser Antilles after the capture of St Lucia from the French in the previous year.

The 350-ton ship *Bellona* was built at Whitby in 1775[67]. Her managing owner was Charles Jackson, who was also master when she was taken into service in December 1777 as a transport and was fitted with at least 153 bunks. In February 1778, with John Wardill as master, she was at Harwich whence she sailed to New York and then to Jamaica. Thomas Woodhouse, mate from January 1778, took over as master in July 1779 at New York, a post he held for the next two years.

The 320-ton ship *Elizabeth* was built at Whitby in 1765. She was one of the transports which took men of von Reidesel's Brunswicker regiment to Canada in 1776. At that time she was owned by Margaret Campion's uncle Thomas Holt, and his son Joseph (then 25) was master. On her return journey *Elizabeth* left New York for Deptford on 17 February 1777 with soldiers from 14th Regiment. From then up to 1779 she was in the

---

[66] I am indebted to John Sands from whose thoroughly researched book *Yorktown's Captive Fleet* has provided much of the information in this section.

[67] Muster rolls exist for the ship from 1775. Lloyds Register, not renowned for its accuracy in this period, gives the year she was built as 1777.

Victualling Service captained by the 28-year old Levi Preston, formerly of *Garland*[68]. She is reported to have reached Portsmouth from New York in January 1779, and in June of that year she arrived at Cork in a convoy of vessels under *HMS Lenox*. In 1780 *Elizabeth* underwent *serious repairs* (probably at Cork), and Joseph Holt had become her managing owner; Preston was still master.

Also built and owned at Whitby was the 324-ton ship *Lord Mulgrave*, Andrew Easterby master and John Addison the owner. In 1779 she had brought some 200 troops of the 80th Regiment (Royal Edinburgh Volunteers) from Leith to New York, arriving on 27 August.

The 287-ton ship *Present Succession* was built in Whitby in 1772, owner, and originally master, John Reed. She was surveyed at Portsmouth in 1777 after which she became a transport ship with Thomas Tinmouth as master. She was later refitted and reported as ready for service on 18 Jan 1780; though she was three days overdue on the time allowed for refitting (which would incur a penalty). On 5 August 1780 a large convoy arrived at Kingston, Jamaica, from St Lucia including ten warships and an array of *Transports, victuallers, and baggage ships, attendant on the troops* for what was rather dramatically referred to in the newspaper report as *the grand expedition against the Spanish Main*. *Present Succession* was included in this collection of transports along with the omnipresent *Royal Briton*, both carrying soldiers of Colonel McCormick's Regiment. In December *Present Succession* was at Portsmouth Dockyard again where she was once more refitted, and in January 1781 she sailed carrying troops to Virginia, her master now being William Chapman.

The 321-ton brig *Success Increase* was built in Whitby in 1772, originally with Michael Cockerill as master, and he was probably also the Cockerill who was owner of the vessel. She entered government service in 1775, first with John Jackson as master and then with Michael Teasdale. After an inordinate amount of time at Cork waiting, she eventually sailed for Halifax in August 1776, under the convoy of the sloops of war *Vulture* and *Hunter*. On 5 October they ran into a terrible storm which separated the fleet, followed by an impenetrable 48-hour fog; but all seem to have arrived safely. In 1777 *Success Increase* sailed from New York arriving at London in April. She was at Petersburg later that year, and she was back in the Baltic at Memel and Petersburg in 1778, probably bringing timber, and perhaps flax, hemp and tar for the naval dockyards. Her master at this time was Joseph Saunderson.

Two Brothers, a 359-ton ship, was built at Whitby in 1774, owner Francis Hall. Her master was originally John Hardwick, but by 1780 was Magnus Mariner - previously master of the collier *George & Jane*. In December 1780 *Two Brothers* with Magnus Mariner as master transferred members of the 5th and 49th Regiments from Portsmouth to Cork.

Some of the other vessels at Yorktown could possibly be Whitby ships[69], and the North East was also represented by *Providence*, built at Stockton 1764; *Providence Increase*, built at Scarborough in 1756, and *Shipwright* built at Hull in 1774.

The crucial factor in this stage of the war was command of the sea. The British strategy relied on the Royal Navy, and any transports and troops that accompanied them, to be able to sail where they wanted when they wanted. Unfortunately the entry of the French, Spanish and Dutch into the conflict made this difficult, as the war had been extended into

---

[68] The 300-ton pink *Garland* was built in Whitby in 1759, and taken into service in 1775 when she had cabins for 126 men and 3 officers.

[69] *Lord Howe, Ranger, Providence, Susannah, Concord, Fidelity* and *Harmony*.

the Mediterranean, where the Spanish wished to capture Gibraltar, to India where the French and Dutch had interests, and to the West Indies where all the parties involved (with the exception of America) had conflicting trade and territorial ambitions. British ships and transports had to be refitted, equipped, manned, victualled and sent to three far-flung continents. In addition the war plan now involved the troop bases in America being more dispersed. Ruling the waves was becoming rather tricky, and if the security of the land forces lies in so doing, then it has to be done all the time.

Also the condition of the British vessels was deteriorating. *Teredo navalis*, the wood-boring worm (in actual fact a kind of clam) was an ever-present danger particularly in warmer seas to wooden ships which were not copper-sheathed (a very expensive process[70]). Putting a wooden sheath and covering the hull with tar delayed, but did not prevent, the process which Bruce Ruiz characterized as *death to the ships that cruised the oceans of the world*. Even apart from the damage caused by this malign mollusc, the woodwork, sails, masts and yards all needed regular repair and replacement. New York, the base of most of the British amphibious campaigns during the war, struggled to find the manpower to do the repairwork in the docks, and supplies of raw materials (sails, cord, iron, tar) –all of which had to come from Canada or cross the Atlantic in storeships- were never sufficient.

The British Navy, which had effectively blockaded French ships in Newport after the occupying force abandoned the territory on 25 October 1779, found that it was impossible to maintain, a fact which their enemies were eager to exploit. In 1780, a French army of five and a half thousand men disembarked at Rhode Island under the command of le Comte de Rochambeau. This force joined up with the American soldiers under Washington to form a formidable army.

It is suggested that Washington wished to attack the well-defended city of New York, but was persuaded by the French commander to attack Cornwallis instead; others claim that Washington deliberately spread the rumour that they were intending to attack New York to mislead the British. Whatever the truth of the matter the result was the same: no troops were sent from New York to reinforce Yorktown.

Meanwhile the French Fleet under de Grasse from the West Indies arrived unopposed in Chesapeake Bay and was able to land fresh troops for Lafayette. A British fleet under Admiral Graves arrived shortly after on 5 September 1781 and there was a series of unsatisfactory and inconclusive engagements after which the British withdrew. As a sea battle it may have been indecisive, but for the war it was pivotal. Graves has been called *the man who lost America*, but he claimed (probably accurately) that his ships were inadequate and out-numbered. While he was seeking to bring his vessels up to strength, another French fleet, under Admiral de Barras arrived from Newport, with much needed artillery. The French totally controlled Chesapeake Bay, denying Cornwallis either escape or reinforcement, and the British were powerless in the short term to remove them or to support the army at Yorktown in any other way.

Cornwallis prepared to meet the combined French and American army, throwing up extra defensive fortifications. To prevent the French from sailing up the river and bombarding the town or landing a force on the beach, thus trapping the British pincer-like, Cornwallis sank a number of transport ships to block their approach, a technique used

---

[70] When at the end of the war the Navy Board put up for sale *Supply* and *Sally* (two Whitby-built vessels bought by the government as store ships) the value of the copper used for sheathing was nearly 12% the value of the hull, and exceeded that of the masts & yards by more than 30%.

previously at Newport. Among those sunk were *Present Succession* and *Success Increase*. *Elizabeth* was converted from a victualling ship to a fireship.

The Franco-American army took up positions around Yorktown on 30 September for a siege that was to last over a fortnight. They gradually moved forward until on the 9 October the town was in range of their artillery which pounded the out-gunned British lines with devastating effect. As the fighting progressed some of the transports had their sails stripped to make tents for the increasing numbers of their wounded.

On 14 October the battle became a serious hand-to-hand struggle fought fiercely on both sides as finally the last two British defensive redoubts were captured. Cornwallis' troops, outnumbered two to one, put up a valiant defence, but it became clear that the British could not hold out until reinforcements arrived. Scuttling several of his vessels, including *Elizabeth*[71], to deny them to the enemy, Cornwallis opened negotiations for terms on 17 October. In the engagement the British had suffered 500 casualties, the French 200 and the Americans only 80. The final act of surrender, a well-choreographed piece of drama, probably in reality almost as theatrical as the subsequent paintings depict it, took place two days later. Along with many thousand prisoners[72], the victors gained large quantities of weaponry, as well as possession of all the remaining ships.

The muster rolls of *Lord Mulgrave* and *Bellona* survive at Whitby. The latter simply records the end of the voyage at *Virginia* for the six seamen on 17 October and for Thomas Woodhouse, master, John Wardill[73], mate, and four servants two days later - on the official date of surrender.

The muster roll of *Lord Mulgrave* laconically states *Ship Taken* on 18 October[74]. In addition to the captain, Andrew Easterby, the crew consisted of William Welsh (mate) Robert White (2nd mate), Francis Cook (carpenter) and Thomas Marshall (cook), eleven seamen and two *Parish Boys under 18 yrs of Age* (Timothy Scott and Peter Catnall). The ship, in French ownership, but still with Andrew Easterby as master, and with a crew of 50 British seamen was allowed to carry captured officers and men to New York, who would all be exchanged for an equal number of French or American prisoners. This was also the case with *Bellona*, Thomas Woodhouse, and with *Cochran*, Thomas Bolton, whose complement of prisoners included Cornwallis. They sailed on 5 December, the same day that Admiral de Grasse left with the French Fleet for the West Indies. *Cochran* arrived at New York on the

---

[71] Levi Preston, master of *Elizabeth*, was presumably captured and exchanged for an equivalent French or American master mariner. In August 1783 he was master of the 350-ton transport *Admiral Barrington*, built in Whitby in 1781 and owned by Thomas Hall. This is probably the same vessel which formed part of the Third Fleet which went to Sydney in 1791.

[72] Among the regiments that surrendered at Yorktown was the 76th (MacDonell's Highlanders) which had only been formed in August 1777. They had been shipped from Leith in March 1779, sailing first to Spithead where they joined a convoy for New York. One of the transports involved was Samuel Campion's *Apollo*, John Adamson, who sailed with 177 men of the regiment to Long Island.

[73] Not the same man who was master of this ship in 1778-9, but probably a relative.

[74] James Robinson, seaman, had left *Lord Mulgrave* in order to join the crew of Samuel Campion's ship *Apollo* at New York on 1 August 1781. He may have felt relieved he had made this change when he heard of *Lord Mulgrave* being trapped with the other vessels at Yorktown. Unfortunately James drowned at New York on 6 Oct 1781.

19 November after what Lord Cornwallis was to describe as *a very disagreeable voyage*[75].
Lord Mulgrave's voyage was even more disagreeable as she met stormy weather and had to seek shelter at Charlestown, and it took another month for her cargo of prisoners to reach New York.

Cochran returned to Yorktown where the French used her as part of their force to defend Chesapeake Bay against the British. *Lord Mulgrave* also returned, but went ashore and is believed to have been a total wreck. *Bellona* was recaptured by the British in the summer of 1782, and the 1787 muster roll for *Bellona* has Charles Jackson as master and owner, with his 15-year-old son Charles as a servant. Intriguingly two other servants in the 1787 muster roll are James Milvil (or Milvin) and George Scott both of whom entered on *Bellona* in 1777; the former was discharged at Jamaica in 1778, the latter had been part of the crew when she was taken on 19 October 1781 at Yorktown.

Two Brothers, Symonds, was sent to England as a cartel ship carrying captured sailors who were to be exchanged. After the exchange she was wrecked near Plymouth; the ship was probably a total loss, though what happened to the French sailors aboard who were being repatriated is not recorded.

The transports scuttled at Yorktown have been the focus of a long-term study by a team led by John D Broadwater. One of them, provisionally given the reference YO88, has been excavated and identified as the 180-ton victualling brig *Betsey* of Whitehaven, master Younghusband.

The news of the surrender reached Britain on 25 November, and was greeted with shock. The British forces had suffered a number of setbacks, but had won more battles than they had lost. However, it soon became very clear that they had lost the war. The unpopular government of Lord North desperately hung on to power for as long as it could and longer than it should; but eventually it went and the new administration set about discussing peace terms.

In 1782 Nathaniel Campion's new ship *Peggy* was launched; a ceremony always full of promise and new hope. She was a splendid three-masted ship of 393 tons; 112 ft long and 30 wide with two decks, a forecastle, quarter-deck, and pierced for 10 guns. Nathaniel Campion was the main owner, though it is likely that Thomas Pyman, with all his experience, probably did most of the work of the managing owner.

In her first year she began, as she was to continue, in the Baltic trade and was reported as having returned to London from Riga in October 1782.

William Hustler, the new master of *General Carleton* in 1782, had been baptized at Whitby Parish Church on 3 December 1738, the son of Christopher Hustler (or Husler) and Jane née Johnson who had been married in the same church on 23 July of the same year. Christopher Hustler was a ship's carpenter in 1743 living at Whitby in Baxtergate, which is presumably where the young William was brought up. Christopher had been carpenter on *Diamond* (1751-4), and was on the crew of *Addison* in 1761 when he died at London, leaving his wife *in very low circumstances*. As the only son William found, aged 22, that he had to support not only himself but his mother and his two younger sisters. William was described as a *carpenter* when he married Isabel daughter of Ann and Richard Brown (also a carpenter) at Whitby by licence in February 1765[76]. His sister Elizabeth, 22, married

[75] In a letter to Rochambeau, quoted in Sands.

[76] One of the witnesses was Joshua Kneeshaw, son of Richard. Richard had sailed, as a servant, on *Hopewell* in 1753 and as seaman on *Agreement* in 1760, both times with Samuel Campion, Nathaniel's brother, as master. He was mate of *Agreement* in 1761.

Thomas Willton[77], 28, (also a carpenter) at Whitby by licence in 1767. His sister Jane married in 1770, age 30, by banns to Thomas Thwaites, painter. It is possible she was more choosy, more unlucky or less personable than her sister, but her marriage by banns instead of the more fashionable and expensive marriage by licence suggests that finances had become even tighter by then. William and Isabel had children, Nancy (born 1768), Christopher (1771), William (1775) and Mary (1778). By the time he took over as Master of *General Carleton* he had been a master mariner for at least eleven years, with considerable experience serving as captain of the transport ship *Saville*[78] and then as master, as Thomas Pyman had been before him, of *Valiant*.

General Carleton had been sheathed, probably only with wood. Not only the ship, but also her crew underwent changes. Thomas Pyman had taken some of the sailors with him to *Peggy*, namely the mate Thomas Wilkinson and the servants Isaac and Simon Frankland. The new mate was George Raines or Rames; Robert Clarkson was the carpenter. Nathaniel Stonehouse, Richard Wrightson, John Johnson, John Noddings, William Johnson, Richard Trueman and Thomas Hornby all stayed as servants, and were joined by John Curtis, James Hart, John Noble and John Thompson.

Nathaniel Campion, using the experienced London brokers John & William Wilkinson of New Broad-Street Building, had tendered *General Carleton* as a foreign victualler for 14s *per Ton Measurement* or 11s *per Ton Burthen* on 2 January 1782. This was in response to the Board's decision to take tenders *either by tonnage or measurement as shall hereafter be agreed upon*. However *the Board did not think proper to close with any of the Tenders* possibly because it had not yet decided which method to use. The Victualling Board had traditionally hired vessels by the amount of cargo loaded (tons burthen) rather than by measured tonnage which was the method the Navy Board used, and this had led to tension between the two Boards, exacerbated by the fact that because the Victualling Board needed fewer vessels than the increasingly large number the Navy Board required as transports, it could also offer better rates of pay.

The Navy Board thought that the change of government, and its concomitant change of personnel in the Admiralty Board, would be a good opportunity to press for a change in the system to ensure equal rates for hiring victuallers and transports. On 26 March 1782 the Navy Board sought to persuade the Admiralty to create a level field for hiring as the current arrangements was *very much in the favour of the owners of ships*[79] which was exactly the reason why Nathaniel Campion had offered *General Carleton* as a victualler. Ignoring this dispute, the Victualling Board had already decided to hire *General Carleton* at 11s per ton burthen on 14 January, subject to survey. The ship's muster roll duly records her employment starting at London on 17 January.

---

[77] Two months after his marriage he sailed as ship's carpenter on *Elizabeth*, having previously been on *Olive Branch*. Both vessels were owned by Thomas Holt.

[78] In 1778 he had been responsible for transporting some 260 men of the *Welsh Fuziliers* in *Saville* from Staten Island to Turkey Point (on the northern, Canadian, shore of Lake Eire).

[79] I am much indebted to Syrett's article *The Victualling Board Charters Shipping 1775-82* for this information.

General Carleton seems to have spent the next two months lying idle with no seamen, and also without a cook. During this time she and other potential victuallers were surveyed by St Barbe, Young, Parker and Farmer. Other Whitby ships being assessed at this time were *Hannah*, James Harrison; *Zephyr*, William Middleton and *Rodney*, Israel Hunter. In the associated paperwork Thomas Pyman is still listed as master of *General Carleton*.

At last orders were received and on 24 March William Hustler enrolled a cook, George Borne, and five seamen: William Marton, James Mackie, Charles Reed and Stephen Buckam. They also took on George Morrey as 2nd mate. Finally *General Carleton* had a full complement.

The surrender of Cornwallis on 19 August 1781 at Yorktown had effectively ended the war with America though peace would not be signed for another two years. In the meantime there was the melancholy business of winding down and withdrawing troops from the former colonies. However the West Indies was still a hotly contended area with France and Spain both having territorial claims there that they were not eager to relinquish.

On 4 April 1782 General Sir Guy Carleton (the man after whom the ship was named) was sent to New York as commander of all the British forces in North America, with instructions to withdraw British troops from America and send them to the Caribbean.

However, the main British concentrations of troops (at New York, Savannah and Charleston) had each to be removed all in one action, as the war was not yet over, and to leave a small group of troops behind would render them vulnerable. To remove the entire force in these areas, together with their stores and the loyalist Americans and their belongings was an enormous logistical operation, and large numbers of transports were being collected to sail to America.

General Carleton was mustered at Spithead alongside many Whitby ships destined for the evacuation of the last British strongholds in the United States. Unfortunately on the 8 April Stephen Buckam, after only a fortnight as one of her crew, was *Drown'd* at *Spithead*. He was replaced on 21st April at Portsmouth by George Bollow.

On 23 April 1782 orders were sent to Captain Patrick Leslie of *HMS Preston*[80] to take command of a convoy to Jamaica which would include *HMS Enterprise*, captain John Payne, and *such Storeships, Victuallers and Trade* [merchant ships] *as may be at Spithead bound thither*. The Admiralty chose four victuallers from a shortlist of fourteen submitted, which were *General Carleton*, *Zephyr*, *Three Sisters* and *George*, of which the first two were Whitby ships. The slight easing of hostilities at this stage of the war is indicated by the fact that *General Carleton* reduced its armament from ten to seven six-pounders, but the West Indies was still a battle zone.

At some stage of their journey Preston's convoy will have heard of Admiral Rodney's success. In April 1782 the French Admiral de Grasse, with the ships which had secured French domination of Chesapeake Bay, was in the West Indies in order to join with a Spanish fleet to make a landing in force to capture Jamaica from the British. Admiral Rodney, supported by Admiral Hood, caught up with him between Guadeloupe and Dominica near a group of small islands known as *Les Iles des Saintes* and there won a massive and decisive victory, now known as the Battle of the Saintes. Rodney had taken advantage of circumstances by giving orders for his ships to sail into gaps in the French line,

---

[80] The previous year *HMS Preston* had been involved in the Battle of Dogger Bank against the Dutch. The conflict was fierce but inconclusive, both fleets withdrawing from the fighting. After the battle the Dutch kept their fleet at home, though they did claim to have been the victors.

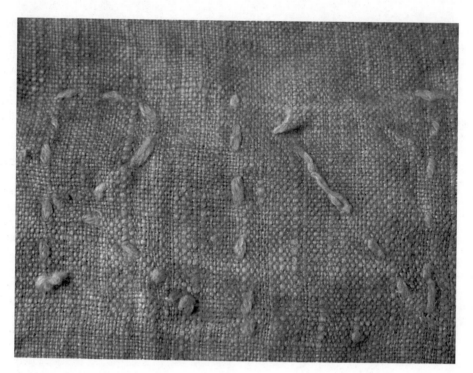

33: Richard Neale used unwaxed sail twine to sew his initials onto this linen bag. The purpose of this item is not clear; it has been suggested that it is a pillowcase, but it is possible it was used to store his private supply of food. Sailors often would bring their own bacon or cheese aboard to supplement the rations.

34: Chamber pots which had been used for cooking. Perhaps an imaginative, and no doubt practical, idea of James Woolf's.

a technique Nelson was to use at Trafalgar. De Grasse was captured along with his flagship *Ville de Paris*.

Not only was Jamaica saved, but Britain had asserted her position as ruler of the waves. It was an enormous boost to the battered pride after the defeat at Yorktown, and a considerable influence on the terms of the final peace treaty.

The victuallers would have been very welcome. Admiral Hood had previously complained that most of the *Bread* [ship's biscuit] that had been sent to the West Indies had *been totally destroyed by the Weevil and obliged to be thrown overboard.*

The work of a victualling ship can be seen from the surviving documents relating to the Whitby ship *Grace*, master William Oxley[81], mate Robert Oxley, presumably his younger brother. She was a 278-ton bark, built in Whitby in 1780. Her managing owner was Robert Burbank, and she was presumably named for his wife (née Bailey)[82]. Other owners were Robert Swales and Christopher Pressick. On 9 January 1781 *Grace* was ordered *to be victualled at Spithead...with all expedition possible* as she was *immediately wanted, for Foreign Service.* The standard victualling allowance for men at sea was (for a mess of six): 4lbs flour or bread and 8 gills of rum per day, and 14 lbs beef, 8lbs of pork, 1½lbs butter, 12 pints peas and 2lbs rice per week. Once in harbour they went on *full allowance*, when the provision for six men was divided between four. Women had the same food provision as men when at sea, but no spirits; when men were on full allowance women had half what the men ate.

Grace victualled soldiers of the 2nd Battalion of Hessian Grenadiers for three periods between 10 September and 9 November 1781. After that *Grace* had been responsible for victualling members of the loyalist Prince of Wales' American Regiment for three periods between April 1782 and January 1783. This covered the period of the evacuation of Savannah on 11 July 1782 which, in Syrett's words, involved *every available transport in America*, and it is likely that *General Carleton* was there too.

It is possible, but less likely, that *General Carleton* was also at the evacuation of Charlestown on 14 December 1782, which required 129 transports and victualling ships, twenty-nine of which then went on to Jamaica.

Loyalist civilians had to be evacuated as well as men of the loyalist regiments. Mainly they went to Canada or to British territories in the West Indies – particularly if they owned slaves[83]. Several Whitby-owned or Whitby-built ships can be identified, with varying degrees of certainty, as being employed in *transporting loyalists, their baggage, provisions etc.* For some we have more details: *Grace*, William Oxley and *Esther*, Robert Gill, both

---

[81] William was born 21/2/1744, son Richard & Hannah. In 1771 he married Martha Shipton, who died the following year. He then married the 19-year old Elizabeth Sleightholm by licence on 20/2/1777. This marriage was declared unlawful *owing to the licence being obtained under the pretence of having the Consent of Elizabeth Sleightholme's Mother, who was not a widow but married again & consequently not entitled to give her consent – as by the late marriage Act.* William & Elizabeth then got married legally and by banns on 2/4/1777.
[82] They had a daughter, also Grace, born 1772, who was to marry John Holt, Margaret Campion's nephew in 1795.
[83] Thomas Brown, the Whitby-born loyalist King's Ranger, settled down on Grand Caicos in the Bahamas where he acquired a plantation of 8,000 acres and over 600 slaves to work on it.

sailed with Loyalists from New York to Canada; whereas *Fishburn*[84], Joseph Gill, and *Royal Briton*[85], Jacob Dunn, transported Loyalists from Charlestown to Jamaica. Although Whitby ships did not participate in the slave trade, during the evacuations of southern Loyalists it is fairly certain that Whitby-owned or Whitby-built ships carried slaves on board. The Victualling Board had its specific regulations for the food allowances for *Women*, *Children* and *Negroes* going to Jamaica. Women and children over ten were fed the same rations as the men, slaves received the same quantity of bread, flour, peas and oatmeal, but reduced quantities of meat, and no butter. Children under 10 were not provided for; and neither Loyalists nor their slaves were permitted any rum.

On 22 December 1782 *General Carleton* sailed from Port Royal in a large convoy protected by the 64-gun man-of-war *Ardent*, captain Lucas. *HMS Ardent* was built in Hull in 1764, and had seen action in the defence of New York and at Rhode Island in 1778. In 1779 she had been captured by the French, and had only recently been recaptured at the Battle of the Saintes. Also accompanying the convoy was the 24-gun frigate *Hydra*, captain Coffin, and the sloop *Vaughan*, captain Burgess. Within a few days of sailing seven of the vessels in the convoy had sprung leaks and returned to Jamaica - an indication of the wear and tear undergone by the transports and victuallers in these waters owing to the rigours of the work and the depredations of *teredo navalis*, and often with little access to repair for months on end. By 4 January 1783 the convoy, by that time comprising 48 vessels, was clear of the Gulf, but their troubles were not over. On the 17th a *heavy Gale of Wind* blew up in some force, scattering the convoy and causing serious damage. The crew of one of the transports, *Swift*, unable to pump out the water fast enough that was flooding in through her shattered hull, abandoned ship and watched her sink beneath the turbulent waves. *HMS Ardent* had been so badly damaged that she had to leave the convoy and make for Antigua, and for a time was believed lost. *Vaughan* had left the convoy to recover a couple of ships seized by a privateer, but after that was unable to rejoin the other ships; she eventually arrived in Kinsale *in a very wretched condition* with a sprung (ie cracked) mast, and having thrown all her guns overboard except two in order to lighten the ship. *General Carleton*, described as a *storeship*, survived the storm and eventually arrived at Cork, going thence to Portsmouth which she reached on 22 February. After no doubt very necessary repairs she made her way slowly to London, and somewhere on this journey, on 12 March, William Marton, seaman, was drowned. *General Carleton* finally reached London on 6 April.

A new voyage for *General Carleton* started on 8 May 1783 at London. William Hustler clearly wished to avoid the problems of the previous year, and was pleased to receive some of the servants whom he had known on *Valiant* in 1780-81 and who worked well with him. These were William Dollin, John Fraiser, Richard Neale, Andrew Moor and John Brion. This haemorrhaging of servants suggests that *Valiant* was lost by this date[86].

---

[84] *Fishburn* was built in Whitby in 1780, a ship of 378.26 tons, owned by Pierson. She was probably never owned at Whitby and certainly was not when she sailed with Robert Brown as master from Portsmouth on 13 May 1787 as a storeship, bound for Botany Bay as part of the First Fleet taking convicts to Australia. She arrived at Port Jackson on 26 January 1788.

[85] *Royal Briton*, owned by Margaret Campion's brother John, was not only at the evacuations of Savannah and Charlestown , but had been part of the fleet involved in the capture of Charlestown two years previously.

[86] The last certain record of Nathaniel Campion's *Valiant* is in the autumn of 1781. She returned from New York arriving at Gravesend on 30 Aug. She was resurveyed and on 25 Sept reported as being *complete in all respects*. It seems likely that she was lost some time between then and early 1783.

Edward Saunderson joined as a new servant. Richard Wrightson left to join Thomas Pyman on *Peggy*; other servants who had left were William Johnson, John Curtis and William Featherstone.

Also from the crew of *Valiant* was James Woolf, cook; what the food situation was like on board *General Carleton* in the previous year with no clear designated cook can only be imagined and the temporary George Borne was probably merely adequate. James Woolf must have had real culinary skills as he seems to have gone straight from being a servant to being a cook, probably even being a cook while he was still a servant: the Navy Board muster for 1780-81 lists him as a *cook* at this time, while the Whitby muster roll for the same period refers to him as a *servant*. This was very unusual, as ship's cooks were usually among the older members of the crew. He seems to have had a gift for cooking; maybe William Hustler enjoyed his food and knew the difference a good chef could make to the unvarying, and often stale or rotten, food that was available to transports both on the long journey across the Atlantic and when based at New York where all food had to be imported. There were a number of cooking-related artefacts recovered from the *General Carleton* wreck, including some chamber pots which, as they were externally charred, had clearly been used for cooking. This imaginative but unusual piece of lateral thinking may have been one of Woolf's innovations, and could have resulted in the ship's stew being more palatable.

Robert Clarkson continued as carpenter. The new mate was John Chapman, with William Dowson as 2nd mate. Nathaniel Stonehouse, having finished his apprenticeship, was now a seaman, and there are two other seamen in William Stoddart and William Campble. Again there was a period of time, nearly a month, between when Hustler and the servants were on the payroll before the rest of the crew were officially on the strength on 4 June.

The entire crew arrived safely back in London. The master and servants discharged on 29 November, and the rest six days earlier.

By then the war had officially ended with the Treaty of Versailles, signed by Britain, America and France on 3 September, though Britain had signed a preliminary peace with the United States in November 1782. The war with the Dutch was in many ways a separate issue and it should really be thought of as the Fourth Anglo-Dutch War rather than anything to do with American Independence; peace between Britain and Holland was not officially signed until 20 May 1784.

Chapter 11

1783 - 5
The Margaret Campion Years

Nathaniel Campion did not live to see the end of the war; he was buried in Whitby Parish Church on 13 August 1783. He was 52. In his will he left virtually all his property to his *dear Wife* Margaret *during the Term of her Natural Life as long as she may remain* [his] *Widow*. This included the house he was living in, presumably the one in Baxtergate, and *also the use Interest and produce of all* [his] *Ships Shipping and Parts of Ships* as well as his *personal Estate and Effects of what nature of kind soever*. At the death or remarriage of Margaret the property was to be divided equally among their three sons and their two daughters. The will is dated 8 July 1783 and the executors are John, Thomas & William Holt (Margaret's three brothers), Christopher Richardson (Margaret's brother-in-law) and John Campion[87] the son of Nathaniel's brother Samuel and Margaret's aunt Jane.

Margaret had been left a widow at the age of 39 with a sixteen-year-old daughter (Jane), another daughter aged six (Ann or Nanny) and three sons aged ten, nine and nineteen months (Robert, John and Nathaniel respectively). She would have had servants to do the housework and to look after the children, though Jane and Ann would have been expected to help while they were still unmarried and living at home. But Margaret would have managed the household, as she always had. She chose never to remarry.

She would have been left well-provided. In addition to having a life interest in the house, and no doubt other investments, there were the *Ships Shipping and Parts of Ships*. This would have included major ownership of *General Carleton* and *Peggy*, and possibly of *Valiant* (if she survived this late), and also shares in *Martha* and *Wisk*. Technically, these ship shares would be in the hands of the executors who would provide her with her portion of the profits when they came due; not a difficult job for them as they were part-owners of the same vessels. However, that was not the way that Margaret was going to do things. Her father and his brother Thomas were master mariners and shipowners. All her father's sisters had married master mariners. Both her grandfathers were master mariners and shipowners, as were her brothers John, Thomas and William. Her sister Elizabeth married Joseph Atty, master mariner and son of the multi-ship-owning James Atty; her sister Martha married Robert Boulby, master mariner and shipowner, and her sister Mary married the ship-owning Christopher Richardson. She would have sailed with her husband on occasion, and possibly sometimes with her parents when she was a girl, or with her brothers as a young woman travelling to London. In many ways she was as much *bred to the sea* as her male sea-going relatives.

Margaret Campion was not, and never had been, the sort of woman who was going to sit in her parlour dressed in fine silks and do nothing but drink tea and gossip with other idle women, while the menfolk concerned themselves with financial affairs. She had managed the family, and now her husband was dead she was also going to manage the family

---

[87] John Campion later became John Campion Coates, a name change that was a condition of his inheriting the wealth of his uncle William Coates who married Margaret's aunt Ann, but who died a childless widower in 1789.

business as well. As for the executors they knew her well, and probably would have expected, and desired, no less. Margaret spelt it out clearly in her own will when she stated that they never *acted in the said Executorship, except in a very few Instances for the Sake of Conformity...the Business of the same Executorship having been altogether...under my Direction and Management.*

Margaret was a firm and robust woman who clearly knew about *Direction and Management.* A likeness of her has survived[88] and though she can not be said to have been pretty, she certainly looks pretty tough. She has a large nose, a firm straight mouth and a decisive chin. By contrast her eyes are large and dark, and though penetrating, are not unattractive. She has curled hair, spilling out from under a white cap. She is wearing a plain dark dress, under which is a white, high-collared blouse. It is difficult to determine the age of the portrait, but she appears to be quite old, so maybe the curls are not entirely natural. One feels that she was not a woman to cross, but that her appearance, when animated, would have had a certain charm.

Fig 11: **Margaret Campion.**

When the muster roll for *General Carleton* was completed on 25 November 1783 it was clearly headed *Mrs Campion Owner.* Right from the start she was going to take charge.

---

[88] In the form of a rather grainy image of a photograph of *a pastel portrait belonging to her great-grand-daughter, Mrs T. H. Woodwark*, reproduced in Browne. The etching which appears here is based on that picture.

She not only managed her late husband's ships, but also invested in shipping in her own right: in 1787 (when compulsory registration of shipping became law) she is shown as being a part-owner of the Whitby-built vessels *Fortitude*, *Jason* and *Sally*. *Fortitude* was a three-masted ship of 313.79 tons, built in 1774, main owner William Benson; *Jason* was a 386-ton bark, built in 1779, 107 ft long by 30 wide with two decks and a poop deck, pierced for 10 guns, main owner Margaret's cousin Joseph Holt; and *Sally* was a three-master 240-ton bark built in 1783, 90 ft long and 26 wide with two decks and a poop deck, main owner Nathaniel Campion's nephew Robert Galilee. Margaret owned 25% (16 64ths) of this vessel.

Interestingly she was not the only woman with similar investments. The Whitby Ship Registers shows that in 1787 Margaret Pearson of North Shields was a part-owner of *Jason*, and among the owners of *Fortitude* were four other women: Jane Yeoman (widow of Thomas), Clara Barker (widow of Peter), Elizabeth Huntrods (a spinster) and Ann Israel (described as *Coal Undertaker* of Shadwell). Margaret Campion became a member of the Committee of Whitby Shipowners, and took an active part in their meetings.

Now the peace was declared, *General Carleton* reverted to her pre-war role, sailing mainly to Norway and the Baltic. Margaret Campion had become a Freeman of the Russia Company, which was necessary for trading through the ports of Petersburg, Riga and Narva. Although *General Carleton* no longer needed her cannon, that did not mean that the ship was defenceless: peace did not mean that the seas were totally peaceable. She had her swivel gun which could be moved to different positions on the deck and, as the name implies, could be rotated to respond quickly to danger from thieves and pirates.

Fig 12: Swivel gun from *General Carleton*.

There were also a number of firearms aboard. A valuable cargo needed defending, and in foreign ports William Hustler would have needed to deal with number of agents, merchants and officials. Some of these may be based at some distance from the harbour, so he would need to hire a horse: his boots and one of his spurs were recovered from the wreck. He would have travelled armed; among the artefacts excavated were several pistols, including a blunderbuss pistol, with a long muzzle, more suitable for a rider than a walker, and which can deliver a scatter of shot to disable the most violent of robbers. However, such pistols did deliver a fierce kick when fired, which made them rather unpopular - so it is something of a rare find.

The 1784 season for *General Carleton* began in London on 10 April. John Nicholson and John Swan were the new mate and 2nd mate. Robert Clarkson remained as carpenter and James Woolf as cook. The servants were: John Johnson, Richard Trueman, James Hart, John Thompson, Richard Neale, John Fraiser, John Noble, Andrew Moor and John Brion who between them had notched up a number of years' service. Nathaniel Stonehouse, formerly a servant, continued to serve as a seaman, being joined by John Dollen who had been a servant on *General Carleton* the previous year and on *Valiant* before that. New seamen were John Growing, Thomas Lee, William Taylor and John Sherwood all of whom were replaced in August, after at least one voyage to Norway, and were probably part of that large and restless body of sailors, many discharged from the Navy at the end of the war, who haunted the docks of London desperately seeking work. Dollen and Stonehouse also left the ship at this time never to return; Nathaniel Stonehouse had sailed on *General Carleton* each season since she was launched when he was fifteen. Servants Andrew Moor and John Brion were also discharged in early August at London; it is possible that their indentures had run their time.

On 24 August Robert Clark replaced John Nicholson as mate. Seven new seamen were entered on the ships books: Ralph Simpson, John Fares, Archibald Camphs (?), James Bower, Jacob Corps, Samuel Hobson and Alex Duncan. They were to be as ephemeral as their predecessors, the last two being discharged after a single voyage to Norway on 30 Sept and Corps following them six days later. They were replaced by John Wilkinson, John Bullock and Michael Stephenson on 16 October and after another Norwegian voyage all the seamen were discharged in late November. The rest of the crew were paid off on 5 December according to the muster roll, though the Receivers of Sixpences account has the ship not reaching London until the 18th.

Du Roi had commented on how busy sailors were, with the captain keeping them *continuously at work, of which there is plenty on a vessel, even when the weather is good.* This is certainly true; captains liked to keep their crew active believing that idleness bred laziness and dissention.

The crew were divided into two watches led respectively by the mate and 2nd mate who would have picked men in turn at the beginning of a voyage. Watches started at eight in the evening and lasted four hours. At four in the afternoon there followed two dog-watches, which were of two hours only; this ensured that a particular watch never had the same hours two days running. The master, technically on duty all the time, the carpenter and the cook were exempt from the watches, which meant that in normal circumstances *General Carleton* would have been run by a crew of eight, while the other watch had time for rest and recreation.

One task that was essential was time-keeping: a half-hour sandglass would measure out the day, at each turn of the glass the *General Carleton's* fine bell would be rung, at first once, then twice, until at *eight bells* the four-hour watch was over, and the whole process would start anew. Time on board ship was often measured in *glasses* (ie half hours); the fight between *Content* and the French privateers (Chapter 7) was described as lasting *near four Glasses.*

It was customary to muster all the crew each day at 6.00am, however, and all the crew were needed when vessels entered and left port, when loading and unloading cargo and during times of emergency when the cry of *All hands!* would bring the entire crew up on deck.

It was the master's duty to keep a log of the journey, and William Hustler would have regularly sat down to write the *General Carleton* log. Each page would have been carefully drawn out by hand into columns with spaces for time, speed, course, winds and comments. Each day at sea officially started at noon, and the day's entry would be divided into two-hour slots in which Hustler would record the changes and actions of that period. Ideally he would write up the log every two hours or as soon as conveniently possible after there had been a change in wind or weather. Sometimes it would be done in the evening, perhaps having poured himself a glass of wine, as he dipped his quill pen into the inkwell on his desk-set and started writing in the details of the last few hours, maybe struggling to recall exactly what happened when as he peered at the page before him.

Fig 13: **William Hustler writes up the ship's log.**

The log of *General Carleton* has not survived, but The Whitby Lit & Phil archive has a collection of ship's logs which includes those of *Swallow* (for 1762) and *Henrietta* (for 1764-8). These books give a good idea of the daily work of navigation. They also include references to the tasks which were given in slack times – often when the ship was in dock. Some examples of such entries are:

> *This day people Imployed in sundry Jobs scrap^t our topmast maid* [made] *a mat*[89] *for our fore sails &^{ct}*
> *scraped all ye half and Quarter Decks*
> *people employed in Diverse Jobbs in our rigging*
> *people employed in making sinnett*[90] *and Spinning Spunyarn*
> *unbent staysail and mended it.*

Mending sails was an important and fairly constant task. All ships of any size would carry a spare suite of sails as well as sufficient canvas to do repairs. After a long journey, particularly one which had included facing a fierce gale or fighting off a privateer, the sails on a vessel returning home at the end of a season could look more like a patchwork quilt than the splendidly clean and pristine ones usually shown on pictures of sailing vessels. All the crew would have been expected to know how to mend sails, an arduous business which involved double stitching of the tough canvas. Recovered from the wreck of *General Carleton* were not only sailmaker's needles and cases, but also three sewing palms – this is a leather strip, with a thumbhole, which is fastened round the hand; the palm side being used

---

[89] To prevent the sails from chafing.
[90] Sennit or sinnet; a kind of flat braided cordage.

as a thimble to push the needle through the sailcloth. The one shown in Picture 38 has additional reinforcement.

In the 18th Century the British sailor was a popular figure, the way the British soldier was not. A song entitled *The Royal British Tar*, words by M P Andrews to music by Dr Arnold, was sung at Vauxhall in July 1783 to celebrate the peace and the seamen's part in it. The song addresses sailors as the *Sons of Ocean fam'd in story*, depicting them as being *to ev'ry fear a stranger*, and the nation as *Proud to boast in peace and war, The virtues of the British Tar*. And proud they were, as the royal and merchant navies between them established the power and prosperity which enabled the country to flourish. It is appropriate that the Whitby ship with one of the longest working lives (built in 1752, lost in 1856) was called *Liberty and Property*, as these were twin aspirational goals of the citizens of Enlightenment Britain, and the British tar was crucially important in their preservation.

However, the public preferred their seamen to be at sea. Although the sailor made frequent appearances in song, story and popular prints he was rarely depicted on land except as saying farewell to (usually) his sweetheart and (sometimes) his wife and family. This idealised sailor was brave and patriotic, portrayed as both heroic and sentimental.

The sailor ashore was to most people a strange creature. With his unusual clothes, ruddy complexion, distinctive walk, strange slang and jargon, he was an alien and rather incongruous figure to many, disturbingly unlike the popular image of the British tar, particularly when they were discharged from the navy in large numbers at the end of the war. Unused to normal society, seamen might appear brutal, rude and lascivious, though they could often be shy and diffident outsiders. There were different social norms on a ship, and a crew which had sailed together for some months - or even years- could generate jealousies, antagonisms and fights; but certainly formed a deep-rooted camaraderie and firm friendships. When bachelor sailors made their wills they were just as likely to leave their property to a friend as to a member of their family. It is not surprising that seamen kept together, ashore as aboard, forming their own subculture.

Over 775 artefacts were recovered from *General Carleton*; of these five have initials and one a name on them to identify ownership. The only named item is a 'cut-throat' razor, in its own leather case, with 'George Ashton' inscribed by its owner on the bone handle. This presents a problem as no-one of that name was ever a sailor on *General Carleton*. There was, however, a George Ashton who married Margaret Fidler at Fylingdales (Robin Hood's Bay) in May 1782. There seems to be no record of his baptism or any evidence that he was a sailor, but it was likely that a young man in Robin Hood's Bay would be either a fisherman or a seaman. A pleasing hypothesis is that the razor was a gift from George Ashton to a fellow mariner who was on *General Carleton* when she sank. Margaret Fidler, baptized at Loftus the daughter of Edward, would have been about 29 when she married, and George would probably have been of a similar age. Being a sailor was largely a young man's work, as Peter Earle has written: *Most regarded service at sea as an occupation suited to a particular part of their life cycle and, if they survived, tended to move into other occupations in their thirties or forties, if not earlier*. It could be that George Ashton had decided to take a land-based job, getting married and wishing to start a family, and that he passed on his much-travelled razor to Richard Trueman, of a sea-faring family in the same town, perhaps in the Spring of 1782, when the latter was beginning his fourth year as servant on *General Carleton* and was of an age when a razor might be needed.

Two other items which could have been gifts are a comb (a very useful item with headlice infestation being so common) with a delightful scrimshaw carving of a seal and

121

some fish, and a woollen stocking[91] (extra stockings were always welcome), both with the initial 'TH'.

Fig 14a: Comb with seal scrimshaw.

Fig 14b: The other side of the comb with the initials 'TH', probably for Thomas Hornby.

There were two people with these initials who sailed on *General Carleton*: Thomas Harrison and Thomas Hornby. The former stayed for a single season, aged 14, in 1778. The

---

[91] Babits and Brenkle have suggested that the initials could originally have been IH, as there are loose threads at the base of the 'T'. This would make it the property of John Fraiser. However the cross-stroke of the 'T' is much wider than the 'I' on his initials on his comb.

latter, a more likely contender, was a servant on board the ship from 1779 to 1783. John Johnson and Richard Trueman both started their time on *General Carleton* in 1779 with Thomas Hornby, and both were still part of the crew at the time of the wreck. It seems likely then that the comb and stockings (presumably originally a pair) were given to one of them as a token of their friendship which had been built up over five years of shared learning, dangers and fun. It is possible that Hornby had finished his apprenticeship when he left *General Carleton* at the end of the 1783 season, and the vicissitudes of a seaman's life were such that there was no guarantee when, if ever, they would meet again.

Of interest is another comb with two sets of initials: 'WS' on one side and 'IF' on the other:

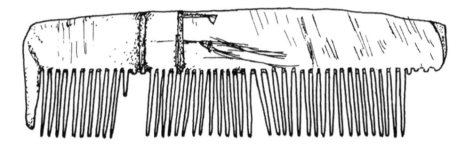

Fig 15a: Comb initialled 'IF', probably belonging to John Fraiser.

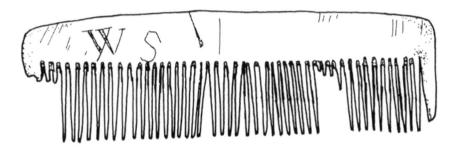

Fig 15b: The reverse of the same comb, initialled 'WS'. A gambling debt?

The capital letter 'J' was usually written 'I' at that time, so 'IF' is almost certainly John Fraiser who would have been its owner at the time of the wreck, but 'WS' is a mystery. There was a William Stoddart who was a seaman on *General Carleton*, but as he was probably from London and only on the ship for less than six months it is unlikely - but not impossible - that a friendship was struck up at that time, perhaps William helped the young apprentice and became something of a mentor. Another possibility is that it was not a gift, but something Fraiser had won from Stoddart in a game of dice. Gambling was one of the ways in which sailors customarily passed what little free time they had on board. Of course 'WS' could be the initials of John's girlfriend back at Whitby. Fraiser was also the owner of a penknife similarly engraved with his initials.

35: Blunderbuss pistol, probably William Hustler's.

36: Sandglasses recovered from *General Carleton*.

37: William Hustler's desk set, with inkwells.

38. Sewing palm, crucial for mending sails.

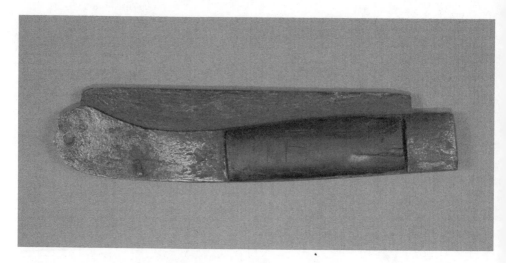

39: John Fraiser's initialled penknife.

40: *General Carleton's* cargo of iron bars lies on the Baltic seabed.

Sometimes the ship's log would record *No Work Done*, when sailors were free to do much as they liked. In addition to gambling and drinking, there might also be smoking. Smoking was a common, if somewhat expensive, pastime of all classes in the 18th Century – and was particularly associated with sailors. Found in the *General Carleton* wreck were some clay pipe fragments, including three pipe bowls - one of which has been identified by Joanna Dąbal from the maker's mark as being manufactured in 1784 by either James Fitzgerald of Chester or John Fearn of Nottinghamshire. Pipes had a short life and would be thrown overboard when broken, so one would expect that the pipes on board to have been of fairly recent manufacture. Also recovered were two smart copper pipe lids which would suggest that they would belong to the captain, mate, carpenter or one of the apprentices from a fairly affluent family. Only one of the pipe bowls showed signs of having been used; as fire at sea was a major fear, when and where the crew were permitted to smoke was restricted.

Fig 16: Sailor dancing to the fife.

Dancing was also a common way for sailors to enjoy themselves. As there were no women on board merchant ships[92] and space was limited, seamen's dances did not involve partners and were performed largely on the spot like the hornpipe dances - the movements for which were based on traditional mariner's activities such as hauling on the ropes and

---

[92] As has been mentioned the master's wife might accompany her husband on voyages; but obviously would not dance with the crew!

Fig 17: *General Carleton* at Danzig (Gdańsk) in 1785, shown moored on the quay outside. the building which now houses part of the National Maritime Museum and where the research vessel *Kaszubski Brzeg* docked to unload her excavated artefacts.

shading the eyes when peering out to sea. Much of the dancing on board ship, however, was probably a largely improvised matter of seamen kicking up their heels and leaping up and down in time to the music. It was an unlucky voyage which did not have some member of the crew who could play an instrument, and the fiddle was popular. I suspect a shrewd master would ensure that he always had a musician aboard; this was certainly the case with *General Carleton* as a fife was one of the artefacts found among her wreckage. Music can carry a long distance over the water so in wartime, when enemy ships were likely to be around, music was banned. The seamen aboard *General Carleton* must have been relieved to be able to dance uninhibitedly to the music of the fife now the war was over.

In 1785 William Hustler sailed with a crew largely similar to that of the previous year. John Nicholson had been replaced as mate by John Swan (2nd mate in 1784), there was a new carpenter in John Pearson, replacing Robert Clarkson who had served for the previous three years; among the servants Andrew Moor and John Brion had left, both of whom had served under Hustler on *Valiant* before joining *General Carleton* in 1783. All the other apprentices were as in 1784.

James Woolf, the young master chef, was also on the strength, continuing to make comparatively delicious meals on the firehearth, using the large copper alloy saucepan which was among the salvaged artefacts. He would probably also be called upon to serve William Hustler tea and toast, boiling the water in the master's fine copper kettle and using the toasting fork.

It is likely that *General Carleton* over-wintered in Whitby, and that the above members of the crew ran her down to London where seven seamen were entered on the ship's payroll on 12 April. These were George Oswell, Henry Bailes, William Clark, Thomas Wooland, Benjamin Moore, Thomas Simpson, William Bailies and Lancelot Malson.

Unlike 1784, when she seemed to voyage only to Norway, in 1785 *General Carleton* was trading in the Baltic. The ship left London on, or shortly after, 17 April, arriving at Elsinore on the 26th, and then sailing to Danzig. Although not as popular as Memel, Petersburg and Riga, Danzig was a favoured port with some Whitby ships, though this is the first recorded visit of *General Carleton*.

Fig 18: Paintbrush recovered from *General Carleton*

She was back in Gravesend on 18 June and discharged her seven seamen at London on 22 June. There was a period of some weeks while the cargo was unloaded and processed with the appropriate paperwork. There would be plenty of minor repair work and caulking for John Pearson, the carpenter. Several of the tools (and parts of tools) he would have used were recovered: a carpenter's square, folding ruler, axe, chisel, hammer, saw, caulking irons, maul, adze, crowbar, augers, gimlets[93], chisel and mallets. The servants would have been busy too mending, cleaning and painting. One of the stockings found in the wreck had a dab of red paint just above the ankle, which could be a result of a bit of carelessness at this time; a much-used paintbrush was also recovered.

On 14 July she enlisted six new seamen: Nicholas Theaker, George Taylor, John Purvis, Andrew Gibson, Andrew Noble and Thomas Edes. Why Hustler thought he only needed six seamen to replace the seven he had recently discharged is not clear, perhaps the year's expenses had been unusually high and he wished to economise: the post-voyage reporting to Margaret Campion could no doubt be quite daunting if she felt he had overspent.

General Carleton reached Elsinore on 22 July, possibly sailing again to Danzig once more. On 30 August she was at Stockholm, where she was loaded with 230 heavy lasts of iron which she took back to London. In September she was back at Elsinore bound for Stockholm once more, where she was to take on a cargo of iron bars and barrels of Swedish pine tar...

---

[93] Some of the gimlets have maker's marks. One has 'PARSONS' on one side of the handle and 'P' on the other. Another has 'HAWTHORN' on the handle and two others have 'HV'. So far the provenance of these items has not been traced.

Chapter 12

Post 1785
Epilogue

After William Hustler drowned, a document was drawn up, dated 8 March 1786, giving the administration of *the Person & Portion* of his son William, then ten years old, to the boy's two widowed grandparents Jane Hustler and Ann Brown who would have been 72 and 82 respectively. This must mean that his wife had died, but the record of that has not yet been found.

William's estate was valued in a brief inventory:

	£	s	d
Personal Apparel	10	10	0
Plate Linnen & household Goods	10	0	0
Money out upon Interest	400	0	0
[Total]	£420	0	0

This would be about £450,000 in modern money and went to young William as next of kin, the two grandparents taking oath that they would administer this money in order to *well and faithfully Educate and bring up* their grandson William, providing him with *sufficient of Meat, drink, Cloaths, and other Necessaries agreeable to his Condition or Estate, during his minority* and also to *save, defend and harmless keep him.*

The inventory was made by Henry Clarke Junior and William Hustler, who also acted as sureties. The document is signed very shakily by Ann Brown, Jane Hustler makes her mark, and Henry Clarke and William Hustler also add their signatures. This William Hustler, also a master mariner, was, probably, the cousin of the deceased.

William Hustler had been financially supporting his mother, and that had now stopped. Consequently she submitted a petition to Trinity House in September 1787[94] and received a pension of 4 shillings per month (worth about £2,500 pa today) from February 1788. Ann Brown died in March 1789, leaving Jane Hustler in sole charge of the boy. Jane died in August 1789. It is not know what happened to the 13-year-old William. Presumably his cousin took over the administration of his patrimony until he came of age in November 1796.

Thomas Pyman continued to prosper. Ironically the same edition of *Lloyd's List* which reported that *General Carleton, Hustler, from Stockholm to London, is totally lost in the Baltick* also recorded the safe arrival of *Peggy*, master Thomas Pyman, at Gravesend from St Petersburg – on board were Thomas Williamson, mate; Simon Frankland, seaman; Isaac Frankland and Richard Wrightson, servants – all of whom had previously sailed on *General Carleton*. Pyman sailed to Norway and the Baltic as master of *Peggy* for many more years, at least until 1797, by which time Britain was once more at war with France, and *Peggy* had 10 guns. It is not quite clear what happened over the next few years but in

---

[94] The petition is supported by John Campion, William Holt, S Pressick, Benjamin Gowland, J Hunter, Christopher Yeoman, Joseph Barker, William Middleton and John Dail.

41: The building in Church Street which was the site of Margaret and Robert Campion's Bank.

42: The altar tomb of children of Nathaniel and Margaret Campion. Margaret's tomb is adjacent.

1800, at the age of 64, he was master of *Elizabeth*[95], returning to Hull from Memel with *linseed, timber etc* in September and from Danzig with *balks* two months later. After a career as master mariner which Young claims was 45 years[96], he retired from the sea and served as harbour-master of Whitby for *several years*, on a salary of £30 per year (about £21,500 today). Pyman's reputation continued to shine: he endorsed Darcy Lever's book *The Young Sea Officer's Sheet Anchor*, first published in 1808. His wife Esther died on 6 May 1803 and was buried in the churchyard four days later. She had lived to see both her daughters (Mary and Esther) married to master-mariners, but had outlived her son Thomas who had drowned at Riga at the age of 23 in 1796. Thomas died at the age of 76 in 1812 and was buried beside his wife on 13 November.

Margaret Campion continued her career as a ship-owner. In 1788 the ship *Fortitude*, Henry Noddings master, was lost, and another vessel of which she was a part-owner, the bark *Jason*, Robert Stephenson, was lost in 1790. In the same year, as a member of the Committee of Whitby Shipowners she was to sign her name to a minuted statement opposing *the new and erroneous mode adopted at Lloyds for classifying Ships* and proposing raising a subscription with the aim of *procuring a correct and impartial Register Book of Shipping to be published annually in London*. There are 38 signatures including hers and that of Sarah Middleton, another female shipowner.

She was still a part-owner of *Sally, Peggy, Wisk* and *Martha*, and had bought a ⅔ share in *Campion*, a ship of 297.16 tons, built in Whitby in 1789, the other owners being her brother-in-law Samuel and his son John. As the century came to a close Margaret was developing other business interests, and in 1798 she disposed of her financial interest in the bark *Sally*, selling an ⅛ share to Robert Galilee, Nathaniel Campion's nephew, and another ⅛ to James Weatherill, possibly Robert Galilee's brother-in-law. This turned out to be timely as *Sally* was lost in 1799.

Margaret's new business enterprise was that in 1800, at the age of 56, she set up a bank in Church Street with her eldest son Robert, who was then 27. In doing this she became, so it is claimed, England's first woman banker. Margaret retired from banking in 1804, at the age of 60. Since her husband's death two of their sons, Nathaniel and John, had died. Only Robert, Jane and Ann (Nanny) survived of the ten children that Margaret had given birth to, the loss of the other seven - three of whom were called Martha - must have been a source of constant grief to her.

Margaret made her will in 1803, leaving everything to be divided equally among her three children, she makes this quite clear, stating that it was her *intention being in Conformity with that of my late Husband, to place all my Children, or have them respectively placed, as near as maybe upon an Equality*. This was so important to her that when it appeared that, by the deaths of her unmarried intestate sons John and Nathaniel, Robert might inherit a larger share of his late father's real Estate than his two sisters, Margaret added a codicil in 1808 *for the express purpose* of stating that if this is the case, and Robert does not make restitution to his sisters to make things equal, then she revokes her bequest to Robert of any of her own property in favour of her daughters that they *may be provided for and made equal*.

---

[95] There are many ships with this name; but the most likely contender in the three-masted, square-rigged ship of 313.29 tons built by George & Nathaniel Langborne in 1793, and owned by John Campion (Nathaniel's nephew) and Joseph Holt (Margaret Campion's cousin).

[96] Perhaps an exaggeration, though it was at least 40 years

Margaret died in 1812, leaving an estate valued at under £12,500 (about £6 million in modern equivalent). She was buried in Whitby parish churchyard on 23 March.

Her son Robert - banker, shipowner and sailcloth manufacturer - was to become one of the richest men in Whitby before his unfortunate bankruptcy in 1842. It was he who, in 1827, erected on the summit of Easby Moor the famous and impressive monument to James Cook who had been a friend of his father and uncles. The inscription reads:

While the art of navigation shall be cultivated among men, while the spirit of enterprise, commerce and philanthropy shall animate the sons of Britain...so long will the name of Capt Cook stand out among the most celebrated and most admired benefactors of the human race.

DRAMATIS PERSONAE

Those Who Sailed on *General Carleton*

Thomas Adamson
Prob bp Hinderwell 11.5.1746, son of Wm Adamson and Sarah née Jefferson. Servant: *Centurion* (1761); Seaman: *Elizabeth* (1768), *Speedwell* (1771); Mate: *General Carleton* (1777-1778), *Antelope* (1779, 1786), *Hannah* (1787), *Lyde* (1788).

John Atkinson
Prob bp 16/10/1743 Wh son Robert Atkinson, sailor. If he is the John Atkinson sailor who marries Sarah Allely, daughter of Francis Allely, 7/1/1766 Wh Lic. then he is well-connected as the marriage was witnessed by Sarah Millner, daughter of master mariner Thomas Millner and sister-in-law of John Holt. Sarah Allely was 18 at the time, and married with her father's consent. Possibly, as a son was born sixth months later, with her father's insistence. Seaman: *Royal Briton* (1775), *General Carleton* (1777); Mate: *Constant Ann* (1781); Master: *Sea Adventure* (1783-4).

Henry Bailes
Seaman: *General Carleton* (1785). Entered at London 12/4/1785, discharged 22/6/1785.

William Bailies
Seaman: *General Carleton* (1785). Entered at London 12/4/1785, discharged 22/6/1785. Poss related to the above.

George Bollow
Seaman: *General Carleton* (1782-3) Entered at Portsmouth 21/4/1782, discharged London 6/4/1783.

George Borne
Cook: *General Carleton* (1782-3).

James Bower
Seaman: *Friendship* (1782-3), *General Carleton* (1784).

John Brion/Bryan
Servant: *Valiant* (1780-1); *General Carleton* (1783-4).

Stephen Buckam
Seaman: *General Carleton* (1782). Entered at London 24 March; drowned at Spithead 8 April.

John Bullock
Seaman: *General Carleton* (1784). Entered 16 Oct, discharged 29 Nov, probably at London.

William Campble
Seaman: *General Carleton* (1783). Entered 4 June and discharged 23 Nov, probably both at London

Archibald Camphs?
Seaman: *General Carleton* (1784). Entered 24 Aug and discharged 27 Nov probably both at London.

Zacharias Campion
Born Staithes, son of Thomas Campion, fisherman (1731-1778) who was a first cousin of Nathaniel Campion, and Jane née Brown; Bap 13/7/1766 Hinderwell. Married

135

Zeboriah Andrew 18/12/1781 Hinderwell. Six children. Servant: *General Carleton* (1778-79); Mate: *Charlotte* (1784-8); Master: *in the Foreign Trade and last in the Active of Sunderland*, serving on which he became *disabled in his right arm* which meant he was *not able to gain his living as a mariner*. In 1808 he submitted a petition to Trinity House, on behalf of himself and his wife, both 53 [he was in fact 41, unless he was baptized a long time after he was born]. They were granted 6/- per month

Cornelius Cayley

Bn 16/10/1764, son of Edward Cayley, attorney at law, and Jane née Simpson. Bp 22/8/1764 Wh. His mother died 1770 & his father marr Mary Brown, brother of Thomas, the *Kings' Ranger*, 1777. Servant: *General Carleton* (1780-1); 2nd Mate: *Silver Eel* (1786); Mate: *Silver Eel* (1787).

John Chapman

Too common a name to identify him with any certainty. Seaman: *Valiant* (1775); Mate: *General Carleton* (1783).

George Clarke

Again a not uncommon name. Possibly the George Clark, sailor, who married Mary Willas 24/2/1767 Wh. Seaman: *General Carleton* (1778-79).

Robert Clark

Poss son of John Clark, sailor, bp 22/3/1752 Wh, aged 13 weeks. Servant: *Royal Briton* (1765); Seaman: *Venus* (1780); Mate: *General Carleton* (1784), *Content* (1787); Master and owner *Mary Ann* (?1791). Marr Margaret Wilson 11/1/1778 Wh.

William Clark

Seaman: *General Carleton* (1785). Entered at London 12 Apr and discharged 22 June, probably at London.

Robert Clarkson

Son of Thomas Clarkson of Robin Hoods Bay. Bp 5/10/1755 Fylingdales. Carpenter: *General Carleton* (1782-4).

John Corner

Son of Miles & Mary (née Jefferson) of Sandsend, grandson of Miles Corner & Catherine née Knaggs. Bap 4/10/1755 Lythe. Married Frances Ellison 3/9/1782 Lythe. Seaman: *General Carleton* (1777-9); 2nd Mate: *General Carleton* (1780); Seaman: *Midsummer Blossom* (1782); Mate: *Minerva* (1786-7), *Myrtle* (1788).

Jacob Corps

Seaman: *General Carleton* (1784). Entered 24 Aug and discharged 6 Oct, probably both at London.

David Coulson

Seaman: *General Carleton* (1777).

John Couling

Seaman: *General Carleton* (1777). Entered 14 May at Hull, discharged 16 August at London.

John Cowerling

Poss the same as above. Seaman: *General Carleton* (1777). Entered 5 Sept and discharged 5 Dec, both at London.

Edward Crimpmore

Seaman: *General Carleton* (1777). Entered 5 Sept and discharged 5 Dec, both at London.

Gavin Cron
 Seaman *General Carleton* (1777). Entered 5 Sept and discharged 5 Dec, both at London.

John Curtis
 Poss son of John and Nihomy/Naomi Curtis, bp Scarborough 11/8/1765. Servant: *General Carleton* (1782-3).

William Daniel
 Bn 29/10/1761, son of Joshua Daniel, officer of Excise, and his wife Mary; bp 10/12/1762 Wh. Servant: *General Carleton* (prob 1777, 1778-1780); Seaman: *Fox* (1786-7). Mar Jane Bradley 1783 Wh; witnessed the marriage of their 21-year-old daughter Phoebe to Thomas Harland, mariner 1806 Wh.

James Dearey/Derry/Dury
 Son of William and Anne of Sandsend. Bp 26/2/1756 Lythe. Seaman: *General Carleton* (1777, 1779-80), *Olive Branch* (1786).

Robert Deighton
 Seaman: *General Carleton* (1780), *Friendship* (1784. Drowned 6/12/1784 Seaton. 2 colleagues also drowned. Owner & Master Cockerill Deighton).

William Dollin/Dollen
 Servant: *Valiant* (1780-81), *General Carleton* (1783); Seaman: *General Carleton* (1784).

John Douthwait
 Married Elizabeth Charter, alias Ragg, widow 28/3/1776 (both make their mark) lic Wh. Daughter Margaret bap 27/11/1778 Wh. Seaman: *General Carleton* (1777), *Lyde* (1778).

William Dowson
 Son of Robert Dowson, mariner, bp 28/2/1742 Wh. Mate: *General Carleton* (1783).

Alexander Duncan
 Seaman: *General Carleton* (1784). Entered 24 Aug and discharged 27 Nov, possibly both at London.

Robert Dunn
 Son of Wm Dunn, *joyner*, bn 1/11/1762, bp 29.12.1762 Whitby. Servant: *General Carleton* (prob 1777; 1778-81); Mate: *Eagle* (1786); Carpenter: *Adamant* (1787); Mate: *Sisters* (1789). Mar Dorothy, dau John Shepherd, carpenter 12/1/1792 Wh. Referred to as Master Mariner in Wh PR entry for the burial of their son William 1800. Probably the Robert Dunn master of the 80-ton Whitby brigantine *Expedition*, owner Robert Dickinson, captured by the French between Hastings and the Thames in October 1805.

Thomas Edes
 Seaman: *General Carleton* (1785). Entered 14 July prob at London. A member of the crew of *General Carleton* when she sank 27/9/1785.

John Fares
 Seaman: *General Carleton* (1784), *Diligence* (1787).

John Featherstone
 Son of Francis Featherston, mariner later master mariner, and his wife Mary née Hogg. Bn 13/3/1761, bp 29/4/1761 Wh. Servant: *Valiant* (1776), *General Carleton* (prob 1777, 1778-80); 2nd Mate: *General Carleton* (1781); Mate *Jason* (1786); Master *Elizabeth & Ann* (1787).

William Featherstone
 Servant: *General Carleton* (1782-3).

James Forbes

Seaman: *General Carleton* (1780). Entered prob Jun 15, discharged 25 Nov.

John Fraiser/Frazer

Servant: *Valiant* (1780-1); *General Carleton* (1783-5); Seaman: *Two Brothers* (1787). A member of the crew of *General Carleton* when she sank 27/9/1785. His comb and penknife, both initialled, were excavated from the wreck.

Jacob Francis

Bachelor & mariner married Ann Garbut* 14/3/1776 Wh banns. Servant: *Royal Briton* (1764-5); Seaman: *General Carleton* (1777), *Mackerel* (1787).

Isaac Marwood Frankland

Bn 21/9/1766, son of Richard Frankland, sailor and master mariner, and Mary, dau of Isaac Marwood, master mariner. Bp 20/1/1767 Wh. Servant: *General Carleton* (1780-1), *Peggy* (1785); Seaman: *Henrietta* (1786); Boatsteerer: *Harpooner* (1787-8).

Simon/Simeon Frankland

Son of William Frankland, sailor and mate. Poss bp June 1762 Hinderwell. Servant: *General Carleton* (1778-81); Mate: *Alice & Jane* (1784); Seaman: *Peggy* (1785); Mate: *Mentor* (1787).

Andrew Gibson

Seaman: *General Carleton* (1785). Entered 14 July, possibly at London. A member of the crew of *General Carleton* when she sank 27/9/1785.

John Goodwin

Seaman: *Volunteer* (1774-5), *General Carleton* (1777).

John Grey

A fairly common name. Poss son of Leonard, carpenter, and grandson of William Grey of Coathouses. Bp 15/6/1755 Wh at 5 weeks old. Seaman: *Royal Briton* (1771), *Olive Branch* (1776), *General Carleton* (1777), *Henrietta* (1786); Linemanager: *Marlborough* (1787).

John Growing

Seaman: *General Carleton* (1784). Entered 10 April at London and discharged 6 Aug, probably also at London.

Andrew Harrison

Prob son of Andrew Harrison and Elizabeth née Storm of Robin Hoods Bay. Bp 6/4/1766 Fylingdales. Servant: *General Carleton* (1779); Seaman: *John* (1784); Mate: *Endeavour* (1786). Could be the Andrew Harrison, master of *Nautilus* captured 1808, prisoner until 1814.

Thomas Harrison

There are far too many possible Thomas Harrisons to suggest a single one with any confidence. Servant: *General Carleton* (1778).

James Hart

Poss son of Thomas and Mary née Pattison of Glaisedale, bp 10/4/1768 Fylingdales. Servant: *General Carleton* (1782-5); Seaman: *Unity* (1786), *Joseph and Hannah* (1787-8). There was a Thomas Hart seaman on *Royal Briton* (1781-84) who may have been his father. James was a member of the crew of *General Carleton* when she sank 27/9/1785.

William Hebron

Prob William, son William, bp 8/9/1728 Liverton. Mate: *Speedwell* (1760); Master *Speedwell* (1765); Mate: *Royal Briton* (1766-67); *Dorothy & Catherine* (1768); *Valiant* (1776); Seaman: *General Carleton* (1779); Cook: *Recovery* (1787 March-May), *Whitby* (1787 Oct-Dec). Bur Wh 23/5/1812.

Samuel Hobson
Seaman: *General Carleton* (1784). Entered 24 Aug and discharged 30 Sept, probably both at London.

Isaac Hornby
Servant: *General Carleton* (poss 1777, 1778); Mate: *John* (1784).

Thomas Hornby
Servant: *General Carleton* (1779-83). Poss the original owner of initialled comb and stocking.

William Hustler
Son of Christopher, mariner and carpenter, and Jane* née Johnson, who marr 23/7/1738 Wh banns. Christopher seems to have come originally from Thornton, and was living in Baxtergate, Whitby, by 1743. He was carpenter on *Diamond* (1751-4) and on the crew of *Addison* in 1761 when he died at London, leaving his wife *in very low circumstances*. Their oldest child and only son William was bap 3/12/1738. William was described as a *carpenter* in when he married Isabel (dau Richard Brown, carpenter, and Ann) 12/2/1765 Wh lic. Master mariner (by 1771), living in Church Street (1778). Master: *Saville* (1775-8), *Valiant* (1779-81), *General Carleton* (1782-5). Drowned 27 September when ship sank.

John Hutchinson
Prob son John Hutchinson, carpenter, bp 11/2/1750 Wh. In the year his son was born, the 25-year-old father sailed with James Cook on *Mary* on which voyage he had the *misfortune to crush two of his Fingers*. The son was a carpenter and seaman on several *ships in the Coal, Coasting, Baltic and Greenland Trade*. Carpenter: *Volunteer* (1773-5); Seaman: *General Carleton* (1777). Also sailed on *Providence and Nancy, Prince George* and *Favourite*. Marr Ann Waters sp 26/12/1775 Wh lic. Children: Jane (bn 1778) and Elizabeth (1780-81). Died 8/1/1786. Widow submitted a Trinity House Petition 14/9/1787 which was signed by (among others) Samuel Campion and John Holt, received 3/- a month for her and 1/- for Jane.

John Johnson
Bn 28/6/1766, son of John Johnson, carpenter, and Ann née Dalton; bp 20/7/1766 Wh. Servant: *General Carleton* (1779-85); Carpenter *Friends Goodwill* (1787-9); Mate: *Henry* (1793); Master: *Sea Adventure* (1794, 1796, 1798-9). A member of the crew of *General Carleton* when she sank 27/9/1785.

William Johnson
Bn 27/1/1765 son of John Johnson, joyner, and Ann née Dalton, older brother of above. Marr Jane Alsop, dau Wm (taylor) & Jane, 7/12/1791 Wh. Children Mary (1800), Susanna (1803) & Edward Alsop (1806). Servant: *General Carleton* (1780-3); Seaman: *Sea Adventure* (1784); Mate: *Sea Adventure* (1787), *Thalia* (1800); Master: *Adventure* (for 7 Years). Lost in *Adventure* in *the Western Ocean*. Widow made petition to Trinity House (1810).

Thomas Lee
Seaman: *General Carleton* (1784). Entered 10 April at London, discharged 6 Aug, probably also at London.

George Littlefair
Bn c1762, prob son of George Littlefair, master mariner. Married Frances Hodgson* 7/1/1787 Wh; children: Ann, Thomas & George, the latter two dying in infancy. George himself died as a seaman on *Favourite* of London on a voyage to the West Indies. His widow submitted a petition to Trinity House in 1794, stating that she is *in a poor State of*

Health and afflicted with Sore Eyes so that she was not able to support herself and her 6 yr old daughter Ann. She received 3/- per month. Servant: *General Carleton* (1778; 1780-1); Boatsteerer: *Marlborough* (1787); Linemanager: *Volunteer* (1789).

James Mackie
Seaman: *General Carleton* (1782-3). Entered 24/4/1782 and discharged 6/4/1783, both at London.

Lancelot Malson
Seaman: *General Carleton* (1785). Entered 12 April at London, discharged 22 June possibly also at London.

William Marton
Seaman: *General Carleton* (1782-1783); entered 24/3/1782, probably at London; drowned 12/3/1783.

Benjamin Moore
Seaman: *General Carleton* (1785). Entered 12 April and discharged 22 June, probably both at London.

Andrew Moor
Servant: *Valiant* (1780-1), *General Carleton* (1783-4).

Samuel Moor
Seaman: *General Carleton* (1777).

George Morrey
Mate: *General Carleton* (1782-3). Seaman: *Friendship* (1787), *Adventure* (1792).

Richard Neale
Servant: *Valiant* (1780-1), *General Carleton* (1783-5). A member of the crew of *General Carleton* when she sank 27/9/1785. The linen bag initialled 'RN', which was excavated from the wreck, belonged to him.

John Nicholson
Poss son of John, sailor, and Jane, bp 27/8/1749 Wh. Married Tomasin Batmison sp 10/3/1778 Wh banns. One of the witnesses was William Gray, sailor, brother to John Gray (seaman on *General Carleton* 1777) who had married the previous year with Tomasin Batmison as a witness. Mate: *General Carleton* (1784): Seaman: *Wisk* (1787); Mate: *Vigilant* (1792).

James Nixon
Seaman: *General Carleton* (1780). Entered 24 March at Hull. Impressed at sea 25 May.

Andrew Noble
Seaman: *General Carleton* (1785). Entered 14 July, probably at London. A member of the crew of *General Carleton* when she sank 27 Sept.

John Noble
Poss son of John, sailor, and Jane, bp 7/8/1771, but this would mean he was only 10 when he went to sea. Servant: *General Carleton* (1782-5). A member of the crew of *General Carleton* when she sank 27 Sept.

John Noddings
Son of John, *mate and carpenter for 40 years*, and Hannah née Sneaton. Bn 5/9/1764, bap 21/10/1764 Wh. Servant: *General Carleton* (prob 1777, 1778-83); Master: *Advice* (1787), *Providence* (1790-3). His father had died on *Providence*, owned by Charles Noddings, 14/2/1789 by *a fall from the Topsail*. Married to Mary. Prob died 29/11/1820, bur 3/12/1820 Wh, but MI transcript has his age as 52 (should be 56) and wife's name as Margaret.

George Oswell

Seaman: *General Carleton* (1785). Entered 12 Apr at London. A member of the crew of *General Carleton* when she sank 27 Sept.

William Parker

Cook: *General Carleton* (1777-9). Died Hull 21/3/1779.

William Pattison

Poss son of Wm bp 17/6/1759 Newcastle, *abode* is given as Sunderland in 1786 muster roll. Seaman: *General Carleton* (1781), *Aurora* (1786), *William & Ann* (1787); 2nd Mate *Sisters* (1789).

John Pearson

Prob son Francis, sailor, bp 27/12/1750 Wh. Seaman: *Thomas and Alice* (1774); Mate: *Friends Goodwill* (1778), Carpenter: *Martha* (1781-2), *General Carleton* (1785), *Friends Goodwill* (1786). A member of the crew of *General Carleton* when she sank 27 Sept.

John Purvis

Poss son Robert and Susanna, bp Newcastle 12/1/1746. Seaman: *General Carleton* (1785). Entered 14 July, probably at London. A member of the crew of *General Carleton* when she sank 27 Sept.

Thomas Pyman

Son of Thomas and Elizabeth née Sneaton. Bp 4/1/1736 Wh. Apprentice to Adam Boulby. Marr Esther Williamson 9/12/1759 Wh lic. Mate: *Whitby* (1758); Master: *Whitby* (1760-1764), *Dorothy & Esther* (1767-1772), *Valiant* (1773-1776), *General Carleton* (1777-1781), *Peggy* (1785-97). Later Harbour master. Children: Elizabeth (1761-3), Thomas (1764-1766), Mary (1767-1855, marr Wm Robson, master mariner 1793), Esther (bn 1770, marr 14/1/1794 Wm Fardon Master mariner), Thomas (1773-1796). Thomas' wife, Esther d 6/5/1803, bur Wh 10/5/03, aged 67; Thomas bur Wh 13/11/1812.

Isaac Raine

Son George and Isabel née Ward of Sandsend. Bp 15/11/1755 Lythe. Seaman: *General Carleton* (1777).

George Raines (?Rames)

This could be the brother or father of the above. Another brother, William, is listed variously as *Rain, Rayne* and *Rains* in the muster rolls. Mate: *General Carleton* (1782-3).

Charles Reed

Seaman: *General Carleton* (1782-3). Entered 24 March and discharged 6 April, both at London.

Nicholas Robinson

Son Richard Robinson, sailor, bn 19/9/1743. Bp 26/2/1744 Wh. Mar Mary Backhouse, daughter of William and Mary née Hill of Lythe, 22/11/1765 Wh. Seaman: *Speedwell* (1766); 2nd Mate: *General Carleton* (1777). His son Nicholas, bn 1769, servant *Diligence* (1786).

Francis Rowntree

Mar Susannah Backas 1/2/1774 Wh (both made their mark). Seaman: *John & Dorothy* (1776), *General Carleton* (1777). Entered Hull 14 March. *Fell from ye main Shrouds in Riga bay & was Drounded* 27/5/1777. Widow Susanna Rountree had two illegitimate children: Snowdon bur 19/3/1781 Wh 1 yr old, Susannah bp 16/7/1781 Wh. Francis' marriage was witnessed by another Francis Rowntree, possibly his father, who may have been the Francis Rowntry, late master mariner, who was admitted as a pensioner of the

Whitby Seaman's Fund in 1786 as being *unable to work*, and was buried as Francis Rowantree, sailor, poor, in 1791 at the age of 52.

William Rudd
Son Thomas, sailor, and Ann née Jackson Bp 30/11/1746 Wh. Seaman: *General Carleton* (1777); 2nd Mate: *General Carleton* (1778); Mate: *Diligence* (1786), *Concord* (1787); Master: *William & Mary* (1788).

Edward Sanderson
Servant: *General Carleton* (1783).

Alexander Schoner?
Seaman: *General Carleton* (1777). Entered 5 Sept and discharged 5 Dec, both at London.

John Sherwood
Seaman: *General Carleton* (1784). Entered 10 Apr at London, discharged 6 Aug, probably at London.

Ralph Simpson
Seaman: *General Carleton* (1784). Entered 24Aug and discharged 27 November, probably both at London.

Thomas Simpson
Seaman: *General Carleton* (1785). Entered 12 April at London and discharged 22 June, probably also at London.

Francis Stephenson
Seaman: *Constant Mary* (1774), *General Carleton* (1781); Cook: *Peggy* (1785-6), *Lark* (1787). *Born/abode* given in 1787 muster roll as Kirby Moorside.

Michael Stephenson
Seaman: *General Carleton* (1784). Entered 16 Oct and discharged 29th Nov, probably both at London.

George Stockton
Born 12/3/1761, son of Isaac Stockton, master mariner, and Elizabeth née Cock. Bp 14/6/61 Lythe. Servant: *General Carleton* (prob 1777, 1778-9).

William Stoddart
Seaman: *General Carleton* (1783). Entered 4 June, discharged 23 Nov at London.

Nathaniel Stonehouse
Born Staithes, son of John and Sarah née Crabtree. Bp 8/1/1762 Hinderwell. His grandfather John Stonehouse married Elizabeth Campion, prob Nathaniel Campion's aunt. Servant: *General Carleton* (1777, 1778-83); Seaman: *General Carleton* (1783-4). His brother James married Alice Jefferson; his uncle (also Nathaniel Stonehouse) was a sailor who fell on hard times and made a petition to Trinity House in 1794; the petition is signed, among others, by Anthony Jefferson.

Thomas Stonehouse
Poss son of Thomas and Mary née Horsley. Bp 12/4/1761 Lythe. Seaman: *Antelope* (1779), *General Carleton* (1781), *Essay* (1783), *Elizabeth* (1787-8).

John Swan
2nd Mate: *General Carleton* (1784); Mate: *General Carleton* (1785), *Sisters* (1787); Master: *Ann* (1790-6). A member of the crew of *General Carleton* when she sank 27/9/1785.

George Taylor
Taylor is a very common name, there are 5 in the Wh musters for 1787, so very uncertain. Poss son of William Taylor, sailor, bp 24/8/1755 Wh. Seaman: *Speedwell* (1777), *General Carleton* (1785). A member of the crew of *General Carleton* when she sank 27/9/1785.

William Taylor
Poss older brother of above George, bp 11/3/1750 Wh. Seaman: *Dorothy & Esther* (1768; Master Thos Pyman; Owner Adam Boulby), *Speedwell* (1775-7; Owner Thomas Holt); Harpooner: *Speedwell* (1778); Seaman: *Speedwell* (1779, 1780-2), *General Carleton* (1784), *Harpooner* (1786); Boatswain: *Harpooner* (1787).

William Taylor
Carpenter: *General Carleton* (1777-1781).

Nicholas Theaker
Seaman: *General Carleton* 1785; entered 14 July, probably at London; drowned when ship sank 27 Sept.

John Thompson
Servant: *General Carleton* (1782-5). A member of the crew of *General Carleton* when she sank 27 Sept.

Thomas Thompson
A common name, but poss son of Thomas, sailor, bn 15/8/1753, bp Wh 6/8/1755 (at the same time as his younger brother John). Went to sea at 11 and was an apprentice for 7 years. Seaman: *Speedwell* (1775-7), *General Carleton* (1778), *Desire* (1779), *Pallas* (1782), *Olive Branch* (1784); 2nd Mate: *Content's Increase* (1787); Mate: *Sophia* (master Henry Jackson) for *13 voyages* in the *Coal & Coasting Trade*. Married Dinah Ellerington, widow, 10/1/1780 lic Wh (Wm Gray witnessed this marriage, too). In 1815, living in Baxtergate, he made a petition to Trinity House on behalf of himself, aged 62, and his wife, aged 70. Received 4/6.

John Tolamy
Servant: *General Carleton* (1778).

Richard Trueman/Trewman
Son of Christopher, seaman, and Dorothy née Richardson of Robin Hood's Bay. Bp 24/5/1767 Fylingdales. Servant: *General Carleton* (1779-1785). A member of the crew of *General Carleton* when she sank 27 Sept.

Edward Walker
Son of Jonathan, mariner, of Aslaby. Bn April 1732, bp 29/11/1733 Wh. (He was baptised on the same day as his brother Thomas, and on the day of his father's burial; presumably his parents had differing views about the value of Anglican baptism). Married Margery Jowsey 5/10/1756 Wh banns. Seaman: *Hannah* (1758); Cook: *Prince of Wales* (1765), *General Carleton* (1781). Son Edward, bn 1761, seaman *Good Intent* (1781-3). Widowed Jan 1792, married Mary Coats* 18/3/1792 Wh banns.

James Watson
Poss the James Watson, mariner who married Sarah Hustler 7/7/1768 Wh lic. She was brother to William Hustler, owner of *Rose*, and cousin to William Hustler, master of *General Carleton*. Cook: *General Carleton* (1779-1780). Master (& part-owner): *Rose, on board of which ship he died in the Month of October 1788, on his passage from the Bay of Honduras*. She makes a Trinity House petition 3/12/1789 signed (among others) by William Skinner [brother of her sister-in-law Ann] and Isaac Stockton. Received 6/-.

John Wells

Son of William Wells and Anne née Atkinson. Bp 31/8/1756 Lythe. Married Mary Backhouse 1/12/1779 Wh lic. Son John bap 5/12/1779 Wh, born 21/10/1779. Seaman *General Carleton* (1778); Boatswain: *Liberty* (1783); Mate: *Elizabeth* (1786); Master: *Flying Fish* (1791-1802), *Newbegin* (1803). Was *drowned on Board the Liberty belonging to Mr Chapman of Whitby on the 27th Day of March* 1804. Mary made a Trinity House petition 9/4/1804, signed by six members of the Chapman family, as she had been left *with two children unprovided for*. Received 6/-.

John Wilkinson

Seaman: *General Carleton* (1784).

Thomas Williamson

Poss son of Robert of Ruswarp, bp 8/8/1742 Wh. Poss related to Thomas Pyman's wife. Mate: *General Carleton* (1779-81), *Peggy* (1785-7). Margaret, his wife, died 1793, aged 25. He did not marry again. Bur 2/12/1821 Wh, aged 79.

Thomas Wooland

Seaman: *General Carleton* (1785); entered 12 Apr at London and discharged 22 June, probably at London.

James Woolf

Birth not found. Seaman: *Valiant* (1776-9); Cook: *Valiant* (1780-1), *General Carleton* (1783-5), *Otterington* (1786-9). Married Mary Thompson* 21/11/1792 Wh lic; children: Mary Ann (1793) & James (1796). His widow Mary married Henry Todd, mariner & widower, 19/8/1806 Wh lic. A member of the crew of *General Carleton* when she sank 27/9/1785.

Richard Wrightson

Poss born 14/12/1766, son of Richard Wrightson*, farmer of Kirby Moorside who married Jane Shepherd 17/6/1762 Wh banns, with Benjamin Chapman as one of the witnesses. Servant: *General Carleton* (1781-3); *Peggy* (1785); Seaman: *Peggy* (1786), *Sally* (1787).

Note: Dates in brackets only indicate years for which I have evidence. Entered and Discharged simply mean when they joined and left the ship's crew.

Abbreviations:

*	They made their mark in the register, rather than sign their name
bap	baptized
bn	born
bur	buried
lic	married by licence
marr	married
poss	possibly
prob	probably
sp	spinster
Wh	Whitby; when relating to bap, mar or bur it refers to Whitby Parish Church

APPENDIX 1

Money and Measurements

Money

British money at this time was in pounds(£), shillings(s) and pence(d). There were also farthings (a quarter of a penny) and half pennies. Apart from the demise of the farthings in late 1950s, this continued to be the case until early 1971. There were twelve pennies in the shilling and twenty shillings in the pound. Three pounds twelve shillings and sixpence would usually be written: £3-12-6 (or £3-12-6d). Two shillings was written as 2s or 2/-; two shillings and sixpence was written as 2s 6d or 2/6, and was usually called 'two and six' (or 'half a crown'). Add a halfpenny to this and it became 2/6½ pronounced 'two and sixp'nce haypenny'.

When our monetary system changed to the present decimal one, the pound remained the same, 50 new pence was worth ten shillings (10/-, colloquially called 'ten bob'), and one new penny (p) was equal to 2.4 old pennies (d). However this equivalence was only relevant at the time; to say in the 21st Century that 10 shillings is equivalent to 50 pence is a meaningless comment. What we want to know is what was the old money is equivalent to in modern terms. However this is no easy task[97]. Generally there are two main, but different, ways of calculating this: using the retail price index, and by using average earnings. They differ considerably: ten shillings in 1970 was worth (in 2007) £5.57 using the retail price index, and £10.09 using average earnings. The retail price index (rpi) tells us what the price of a commodity was compared to today's price so, for example, if a chocolate bar cost 6d (sixpence) in 1950 that would be equivalent to our paying 62p today; but if we wanted to know what share of an average person's income would be taken up with this purchase (ie how *affordable* it is) compared to 1950 the chocolate bar would cost us £1.83. The further back in time one goes, the more difficult it is to make meaningful comparisons, as they lived in a world with different retail demands and a different distribution of earnings; at the time covered by this book the average earnings index gives a value in excess of ten times the retail price index value. The retail price index is possibly more useful for small items, but as most of the comparisons made in this book are of larger sums (eg cost of building a ship, value of an estate) I have used the average earnings index. Where sums in old money are mentioned in the text the approximate modern value, using the average earnings index, often appears immediately after in brackets. Sometimes, usually for smaller sums, I have used both values, in which case the rpi is the first, and the average earnings index the second.

Length

The units of length were mainly inches (ins), feet (ft) and yards (yds). 2 feet and 6 inches can be written as 2 ft 3 ins or as 2' 3". There were twelve inches to a foot, and three feet in a yard. A mile was 1760 yds. A fathom, used in measuring depth, was six feet.

---

[97] I have used Measuring Worth on http://www.measuringworth.com. The latest year they use is 2007, which I have taken the liberty of calling 'today's value'.

Their approximate modern metric equivalents are:
1 inch = 2.5 cms
1 foot = 30.5 cms
1 yard = 0.91m
1 fathom = 1.83m

Speed

Speed of ships at sea was and is measured in knots; a knot being a nautical mile per hour. A nautical mile is a minute of longitude at the equator, which is approximately 2027 yds. 1 knot is approximately 1.15 mph and 1.85 kph.

Weight

The imperial pound (lb) is the smallest unit of weight which appears in this book, it is divided into 16 ounces. Cargoes were often measured in hundredweight (cwt) which was 112 lbs; a quarter was a quarter of a hundredweight (ie 28 lbs). 20 cwt made a ton.

Their approximate modern metric equivalents are:
1 pound (lb) = 0.45 kg
1 hundredweight (cwt) = 50.8 kg
1 ton = 1.02 metric tonnes

Ship tonnage

A ship's tonnage is meant to indicate the number of tons of cargo she is able to carry (tons burthen). This is a very vexed question, as much depends upon the type of cargo, and what is, in practice, measurable. For colliers, vessels were rated by the amount of coal they could carry. This was measured in keels; a keel being 8 Newcastle chaldrons (of 53 cwt) or 21 tons and 4 cwt. The boats which ferried coal down the Tyne to Shields for loading onto the colliers were known as keels, because they carried this amount of coal. A list of Whitby-owned vessels in 1773 listed their capacity in keels. This, at least, gave a clear way of comparing the carrying capacity of these vessels.

There were a number of different methods of finding tonnage in the early 18th Century, which caused much confusion. So far as the Navy Board was concerned, being able to measure the tonnage of a vessel was crucial, as transports were chartered at so much per ton; and this need was partly responsible for the Act of Parliament (1772) which laid down an official standard way of measuring ships tonnage. This was: *The length shall be taken on a straight Line along the Rabbet of the Keel of the Ship, from the back of the Main sternpost to a perpendicular Line from the Forepart of the Main Stem under the Bowsprit, from which subtracting Three-fifths of the Breadth, the Remainder shall be esteemed the just Length of the Keel [L] to find the Tonnage; and the Breadth [B] shall be taken from the outside of the Plank in the Broadest Place in the Ship, be it either above or below the Main Wales, exclusive of all manner of doubling Planks that may be wrought upon the Sides of the Ship.* These measurement were then used in the following equation to find *the true Contents of the Tonnage.*

$$\frac{(L - 3/5B) \times B \times \frac{1}{2}B}{94}$$

All vessels measured by the Navy Board would have had their tonnage established in this way from January 1776 (though there was a slight change to the way the breadth was measured in 1781). Here are some Whitby vessels with their capacity in keels and their Navy Board measured tonnage for comparison:

Name	Capacity in keels	Navy Board measured tonnage
Ceres	13	155.37
John & Christopher	20	293.50
Royal Briton	20	303.00
Christopher	21	296.82
Success Increase	23	321.18
Dorothy & Catherine	24	327.85
Valiant	24	341.44
Saville	24	352.44

Although Steel in 1805 described the 1772 regulation as being a *very defective rule* because it meant that all vessels with the same *length of keel and extreme breadth* will *appear to be precisely of the same burthen or capacity* even if *their bodies be extremely full or extremely sharp*, the system persisted. The next dramatic change in standardising tonnage measurement was the Moorsom Rule, in the mid 19th Century.

Volume

Imperial measurements of volume:
4 gills = 1 pint
2 pints = 1 quart
4 quarts = 1 gallon (gall)

Dry measure:
1 bushel = 64 pints

Approximate metric equivalents:
1 gill = 142 mls
1 pint = 568 mls
1 gall = 4.55 litres
1 bushel = 36.4 litres

APPENDIX 2

The Interconnection of Whitby Shipbuilding Families

The inter-relation between Nathaniel and Margaret Campion and other Whitby ship-builders was enormously complex. Nathaniel Campion's brother Samuel married Jane, the daughter of Joseph Holt one of the original founders of the Dock Company; their son John Campion (Coates) and his wife Elizabeth had four children who married into shipbuilding families: Joseph married Eleanor, daughter of Thomas Broderick, Thomas married Alice daughter of Thomas Fishburn, John married Elizabeth daughter of John Barry, and granddaughter of Robert Barry, both shipbuilders, and Emily married Gideon Smales, of the long-standing shipbuilding family.

Not only was Margaret's brother John, and possibly her father (also John), a ship-builder, but so was her brother William Holt who married Mary Lotherington whose uncle was Jonathan Lacy, also a shipbuilder. Margaret Campion's aunt Elizabeth Holt married William Skinner; their son William married Mary the sister of John Holt (another one, Margaret's nephew), shipbuilder; and their daughter Elizabeth married William Reynolds, shipbuilder, son of John Reynolds one of the founder members of the Dock Company, and gt-grandson of Jarvis Coates who, with his two sons Jarvis and Benjamin, were shipbuilders. William Skinner's sister Ann married William Hustler, shipbuilder. Margaret Campion's sister Mary married Christopher Richardson and their two sons, John & Christopher, were not only shipbuilders, but they both married daughters of the shipbuilder Joseph Barker.

Nathaniel and Margaret's children would also become part of it: their son Robert, and his two sons John & William were shipbuilders; their daughter Nanny married Joseph Huggins Barker, son of Joseph Barker, and their daughter Jane married Lacy Lotherington whose uncle was Jonathan Lacy, shipbuilder, and whose sister Mary was the wife of Margaret's aforementioned ship-building brother William. Elizabeth, the sister of Joseph Huggins Barker married Aaron Chapman whose brother Abel was a shipbuilder and was succeeded in the business by his son Wakefield Simpson Chapman who married his cousin Dorothy Simpson, of yet another shipbuilding family...

APPENDIX 3

How Many People Died in the General Carleton Shipwreck?

The simple answer to this is that we do not know.

We do know that there was a terrible storm on 26 September 1785, *Lloyd's List* for 11 October gives a record of *Accidents in the Storm of the 26th Ult* which mentions a number of vessels being stranded – including *Johnan Runken* returning to her home port of Danzig from Portsmouth in ballast. The first account of *General Carleton* being in trouble is one from Elsinore dated 4 October, which appeared in *Lloyd's List* on the 18th, stating: *the Gen. Carleton, Capt Hustler, from Stockholm, was seen this Day Week* [27 September] *in the East Sea* [the Baltic] *very leaky, and it is thought she stood in for Danzick Road.*

Lloyd's List for 21 October reports the sinking of the ship: *the General Carleton, Hustler, from Stockholm to London, is totally lost in the Baltick, and all the Crew, except three Men.*

The muster roll was compiled on 22 February 1787, and it is interesting to speculate who compiled it and from what source(s). It lists all the names of the people who served on the ship with their *post on board*, and dates when they were entered and discharged. It lists 18 men on the ship's payroll on 27 September 1785; but it is not at all clear how many of these, if any, survived.

The problems are to do with the nature and accuracy of the muster rolls and the use of the ditto mark, which looks like a pair of inverted commas. This mark is used in the muster rolls both as a ditto, but also simply as a space-filler; for example it appears under *Servt* and *Seaman* unquestionably as ditto marks to indicate the role on board of the subsequent names. But in the column for *Place of Abode*, the name *Whitby* appears opposite William Hustler's name, but the rest of the column is all ditto marks, but it is not at all likely that all the rest of the crew came from Whitby. The next column, for the crew member's previous voyage, has no information in it at all but is filled with ditto marks which are here used as space-fillers. The muster rolls when Thomas Pyman was master were more clear, writing *Do* for a proper ditto and a kind of squiggle for space-fillers. The ambiguity of the 1785 muster roll makes the interpretation of the column headed: *Time when, and Place where Discharged, Run, Dead, Killed, Slain or Drowned* very difficult. Against William Hustler's name is written *27 Sept 1785 Drown'd*, underneath this the there are ditto marks against the next 11 names (mate, cook, carpenter and the servants), then against the name of George Oswell is *22nd June 1785 Dischd* underneath which are ditto marks in the rows for the other the six seamen who had left the ship then. Beneath that, against the name Nicholas Theaker, is *27 Sept Drown'd* with ditto marks in the next five rows for the other seamen.

The three most likely interpretations of the muster roll are: that all 18 members of the crew were drowned; that only William Hustler and Nicholas Theaker drowned; or that the compiler of the roll did not have any clear knowledge of who had survived and who had not (apart from Hustler & Theaker), and was being deliberately ambiguous.

The purpose of the muster roll was not to record accurate details of what happened to the crew, but to calculate, and pay, the exact money due to the Seamen's Fund. As it was submitted some 17 months after the event, there had no doubt been some pressure to complete the paperwork, and to pay the debt. After all, Nathaniel Campion himself as a trustee for the administration of the Whitby Seaman's Fund had complained about uncompleted muster rolls and the subsequent shortage of money available for seamen's widows and dependents. It is likely that Margaret would have wished to expedite its completion, whether or not it recorded the deaths accurately.

There were no human remains of crew members excavated from the wreck, which might imply that most of them reached the shore, in accordance with the traditional legend told in Dębki. Also, apart from William Hustler's mother, no dependents of the crew members applied either to Trinity House or the Whitby Seamen's Hospital. This is suggestive, but it is unwise to put too much reliance on negative evidence. It must be remembered that most seamen, and all the apprentices, were young and unmarried, so even if most of the crew drowned there may not have been any widows.

And what of the three survivors mentioned in *Lloyds List*? There may well have been more than three. James Woolf survived; and it is highly likely that John Swan, John Pearson, John Johnson and James Hart also did. James Woolf continued to be a cook, starting work in April 1786, on *Otterington*, a 350-ton ship owned by William Holt and Christopher Richardson, Margaret Campion's brother and brother-in-law. No doubt Woolf's reputation for providing edible food was known to them and they snapped him up for their ship as soon as he managed to return to Whitby. James Woolf stayed on *Ottrington* for at least four years.

In 1787 John Swan was mate on *Sisters*, of which Benjamin Gowland was both master and owner. Swan became a master mariner, and from 1790 was captain of the two-masted 123-ton brig *Ann*, which was built in 1787 by Thomas Fishburn and was owned by William Usherwood. *Ann's* ship book survives, and is held in the Whitby Lit & Phil archives; it records a voyage in 1793, with John Swan as master, to London and Danzig, which made a profit of £52-8-9d (equivalent of about £53,000). It could well have been John Swan who completed the muster roll for *General Carleton*.

John Pearson had sailed as seaman on *Thomas and Alice* in 1774, and as mate on the brigantine *Friends Goodwill* (Valentine Kitichingman master and owner) in 1778. He was then carpenter on *Martha*, Isaac Chapman, in 1781, joining *General Carleton* (whose owners were much the same people who owned *Martha*) in April 1785. In March 1786 he was on *Friends Goodwill* once more, this time as a carpenter. He is probably also the John Pearson who was a cook on *Myrtle* in 1788.

John Johnson, who was presumably trained as a carpenter like his father, was probably the John Johnson who took over the post of carpenter on *Friends Goodwill* from John Pearson in 1787 for three years. After serving as mate on *Henry* in 1793, he became master the following year of the 248-ton ship *Sea Adventure* (on which his elder brother William had served in 1784), a post he still held in 1799[97].

James Hart completed his apprenticeship aboard *General Carleton*. After surviving the wreck, he sailed as a seaman on the 253-ton brigantine *Joseph and Hannah*, John Emblington master and owner, in 1787 and the following year.

It is also possible that James Fraiser survived to sail on *Two Brothers* in 1787.

---

[97] By which time the ship was already 75 years old. Young records that she finally met her end in a storm off the coast of Lincolnshire in 1810, when she was driven onto the shore and deposited in the middle of a field *a good distance from the sea*.

APPENDIX 4

Knit Your Own *General Carleton* Woollen Hat

Materials:
One ball of white handspun wool.
One ball of black handspun wool.
One small ball of coloured handspun wool.
A set of double pointed needles of a size to suit your yarn (it is important to make a tension square)

Tension:
I have made this hat with handspun wool, so it is important to do a tension square. My tension was 20 stitches and 22 rows to a 10cm square knitted over the fair isle pattern. Measure the head size required and calculate how many stitches correlate to that size. Round to the nearest number that is divisible by 16. This will be the main stitch count.

Brim
Cast on in white your 'main stitch count' plus a further 16 st. Mark the start of the row with coloured thread.
Knitting in rounds, knit 10 rows.
Purl one row.

Knit the first 10 rows on the pattern chart, starting at the bottom and working upwards.
Next row, fold back the brim wrong sides together and pick up one stitch from the cast on edge and knit it together with the corresponding stitch on the needle for the entire round. This creates a double thickness brim for the hat.

Side of hat:
Next row, keeping pattern correct, make 16 decreases evenly across the round. You should now have your 'main stitch count' on your needles.
Continue the pattern ending on row 37.

Shaping top of hat:

On row 38 (first black section) make 8 decreases evenly throughout the round.
Continue the pattern straight ending on row 47.
On row 48 (second black section). Make 8 decreases evenly throughout round. Knit to the end of pattern.
Change to white.
(Knit 14 dec 1) repeat for the round.
(Knit 13 dec 1) repeat for the round.
Knit 1 round.
(Knit 12 dec 1) repeat for the round.
(Knit 11 dec 1) repeat for the round.
Knit 1 round.
(Knit 10 dec 1) repeat for the round.
(Knit 9 dec 1) repeat for the round.
(Knit 8 dec 1) repeat for the round.
(Knit 7 dec 1) repeat for the round.
(Knit 6 dec 1) repeat for the round.
(Knit 5 dec 1) repeat for the round.
(Knit 4 dec 1) repeat for the round.
Knit one round.
(Knit 3 dec 1) repeat for the round.
(Knit 2 dec 1) repeat for the round.
(Knit 1 dec 1) repeat for the round.
Knit 2 together for the round. Draw up stitches.

To finish:

Make some thrums by wrapping the white and coloured yarn round your hand and cutting them at the top and the bottom. Knot a small bundle and sew these on the top of the hat as a tassel. Using a crochet hook and one white and one coloured thrum make the fringed edge (push crochet hook through bottom edge of hat, loop middle of thrums over hook and pull through the hat. Thread the ends of the thrums through the loop pulled through. Pull the ends tight). Fray the ends of the thrums by combing them. A vigorous wash in hot soapy water will slightly felt the hat and make it thicker and warmer.

Pattern chart:

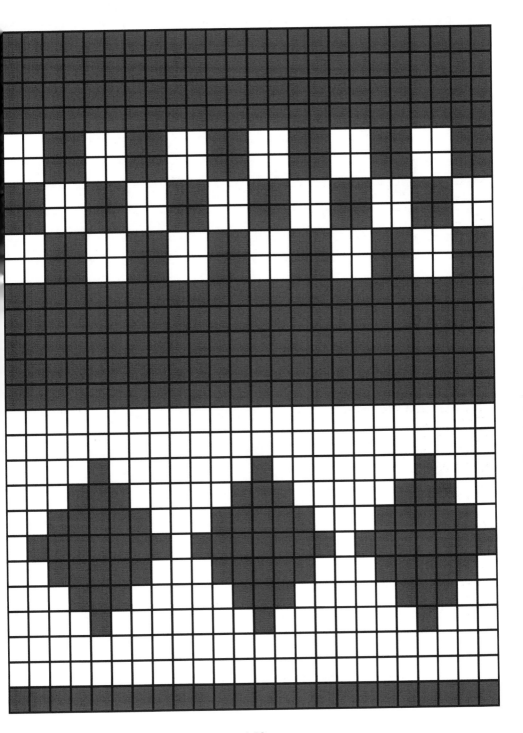

	Key:
■	Black wool
□	White wool
▨	Coloured wool

BIBLIOGRAPHY

Manuscript Sources:
The Borthwick Institute, York: Wills of Nathaniel & Margaret Campion, Admons of William Hustler.

The National Archives, Kew: ADM: 7/565, 49/2, 4 & 6, 68/137-145, 106/3318, 3320, 3405, 3529-30, 3612-3, 111/89-90, 174/295-6; CO 390/5; CUST 90/7; 90/74; E 190 283/3, 286/7, 286/9; WO 60/23.

The National Maritime Museum, Greenwich: SMF 153; and documents relating to impressment.

The North Yorks County Records Office (NYCRO): Whitby Parish Registers, Whitby Ship Registers, Whitby muster rolls

Society of Genealogists (SOG): Trinity House petitions, various parish registers.

The Whitby Literary & Philosophical Society: Muster Rolls; ships' books and logs; Seamen's Hospital documents.

Printed Sources
Abbass, D. K. 2006. *Rhode Island in the Revolution: Big Happenings in the Smallest Colony*. RIMAP.

Babits, Lawrence and Brenckle, Matthew. 2008. "Sailor Clothing" in *The General Carleton Shipwreck, 1785*. Polish Maritime Museum. Gdańsk.

Bagshawe, J.R. 1933. *The Wooden Ships of Whitby*. Whitby.

Bailey's British Directory; or Merchants and Traders' Useful Companion. 1781 & 1784. London

Baines, Stephen. 2008. "The History of *General Carleton*, and of Some of Those Connected with Her" in *The General Carleton Shipwreck, 1785*. Polish Maritime Museum, Gdańsk.

Baines, Stephen. 2008. "The Port of Whitby and its Shipbuilding in the Eighteenth Century" in *The General Carleton Shipwreck, 1785*. Polish Maritime Museum, Gdańsk.

Barker, Rosalin. 1992. *Prisoners of the Tsar: East Coast Sailors held in Russia 1800-1801*. Highgate (Beverley)

Barker, Rosalin. 2003. " 'Tea for the cabin, milk for the boys and butter for the ship'; the contribution of the 18th-century merchant fleet to retail trade in NE England" Paper delivered to CHORD Conference, printed in *Whitby Literary & Philosophical Society Annual Report*, 2004.

Barker, Rosalin. 2007. *Whitby: An Extraordinary Town*. Blackthorn Press.

Barrow, Tony. 2001. *The Whaling Trade of North-East England*. University of Sunderland.

Beaglehole, J. C. 1974. *The Life of Captain James Cook*. A & C Black.

Beresford, James (ed). Blythe Ronald (intro). 1999. *James Woodforde. The Dairy of a Country Parson 1758-1802*. Canterbury Press.

Broadwater, John D., Adams, Robert M. & Renner, Marcie.1985. "The Yorktown Shipwreck Archaeological Project: An interim report on the excavation of shipwreck 44YO88" in *The International Journal of Nautical Archaeology and Underwater Exploration*. (1985) 14.4. pp301-314.

155

Broadwater, John D. 1988. "Yorktown Shipwreck". *National Geographic* June 1998.

Broadwater, John D. 1989. "Merchant Ships at War: The Sunken British Fleet at Yorktown, Virginia" in *Underwater Archaeology Proceedings from the Society for Historical Archaeology Conference*. (Ed) Arnold, J Barto. Maryland.

Broadwater, John D. 1995. "In the Shadow of Wooden Walls: Naval Transports during the American War of Independence" in *The Archaeology of Ships of War*. Mensun Bound (Ed). International Maritime Archaeology Series Volume 1. Nelson.

Brogan, Hugh. 1985 (1999) *The Longman History of the United States*. Longman.

Browne, H. B. 1946. *Chapters of Whitby History 1823-1946*. Brown & Sons.

Campbell, Charles. 1828. *Memoirs of Charles Campbell, at Present Prisoner in the Jail of Glasgow*. Glasgow.

Cahin, Edward J. 1999. *The King's Ranger. Thomas Brown and the American Revolution on the Southern Frontier*. New York

Charlton, Lionel. 1779. *A History of Whitby, and of Whitby Abbey*. York.

Cieślak, Edmund and Biernat, Czesław (Trans Blaim, B. & Hyde, G.). 1995. *History of Gdańsk*. Gdańsk

Davidoff, L. & Hall, C. 1987. *Family Fortunes: Men and Women of the English Middle Classes 1780-1850*. Routledge.

Deane, Anthony. 1996. *Nelson's favourite; HMS Agamemnon at War 1781-1809*. Caxton.

Dąbal, Joanna. 2009. "Tobacco clay pipes" in *The General Carleton Shipwreck, 1785*. Polish Maritime Museum, Gdańsk.

Davis, R. 1962. *The Rise of the English Shipping Industry in the 17th and 18th Centuries*. Davis and Charles.

Defoe, D. 1726, *A Tour through the Whole Island of Great Britain*. London (Penguin Classics 1986).

Earle, Peter. 1998. *Sailors, English Merchant Seamen 1650-1775*. Methuen

Flannery, Tim (Ed). 2000. *John Nichol, Mariner*. Canongate.

Gaskin, R. T. 1909. *The Old Seaport of Whitby*. Whitby

Gould, John. 2000. "The Newcastle Port Books and the coastal trade: the results of a computer based investigation into vessel utilisation and shipping losses in the Eighteenth Century." in *New Researches in Maritime History*. March 2000

Gregory, Jeremy & Stevenson, John. 2000. *Britain in the Eighteenth Century 1688-1820*. Longman.

Harland, John. 1984 (1996). *Seamanship in the Age of Sail*. Conway.

Harland, Joyce. *George Weatherill 1810-1890*.

Hibbert, C. 1990. *Redcoats and Rebels: the War for America 1770-1781*. Grafton (Penguin 2001)

Holt, Robert B. 1897. *Whitby Past and Present*. Copas and Horne.

Jones, S.K. 1982. *A Maritime History of the Port of Whitby, 1700-1914*. Unpublished PhD thesis. London University

Lavery, B. (Ed) 1998. *Shipboard Life and Organisation 1731-1815: Sovereignty of Sail*. Ashgate.

Lemire, Beverly. 1997. *Dress, Culture and Commerce. The English Clothing Trade before the Factory, 1660-1800*. Macmillan.

Lloyds List (facsimile edn)

Lloyds Register (facsimile edn)

MacGregor, D. R. 1985. *Merchant Sailing Ships, 1775-1815.* Conway.

Mead, Hilary P. 1947. *Trinity House, its Unique Record from the Days of Henry VIII.* London

Nivelon, Francis. 1737. *The Rudiments of Good Behaviour.* Facsimile Ed (2003) Paul Holberton.

Ossowski, Waldemar (Ed). 2008. *The General Carleton Shipwreck, 1785.* Polish Maritime Museum, Gdańsk.

Ossowski, Waldemar. 2008. "Archaeological Underwater Excavation of Wreck W-32" in *The General Carleton Shipwreck, 1785.* Polish Maritime Museum, Gdańsk.

Phillips, M. 1894. *A History of Banking in Northumberland, Durham and North Yorkshire (1755-1894).* London

Pocock, Tom. 1998. *Battle for Empire.* Michael O'Mara

Robinson, William. 1836. (1973, with Intro by Oliver Warner). *Jack Nastyface, Memoirs of an English Seaman.* London (Annapolis)

Rodzik, Irena & Jakimowicz, Beata. 2009. "Leather Artefacts" in *The General Carleton Shipwreck, 1785.* Polish Maritime Museum, Gdańsk.

Roger, N. A. M. (Ed). 1998. *The Narrative of William Spavins a Chatham Pensioner by Himself.* (Originally Louth 1797) Chatham.

Roger, N. A. M. 2004. *The Command of the Ocean.* Penguin

Sands, John O. 1983. *Yorktown's Captive Fleet.* University Press of Virginia.

Styles, John. 1994. "Clothing the North: The Supply of Non-elite Clothing in the Eighteenth-Century North of England." In *Textile History* 25 (2) 139-166

Syrett, D. 1970. *Shipping and the American War 1775-83: A Study of British Transport Organisation.* Athlone Press

Syrett, David. 1995. "The Victualling Board Charters Shipping 1775-82" in *Historical Research* Vol 68 Issue 166 pp212-24

Thornton, Cliff. (Ed). 2000. *Bound for the Tyne: Extracts from the Diary of Ralph Jackson.* Newcastle.

Universal British Directory, The. 1793-98. London. Reprinted 1993. Michael Winton

Weatherill, Richard. 1908. *The Ancient Port of Whitby and Its Shipping.* Whitby.

White, Andrew. 1995. *A History of Whitby.* Phillimore.

Willan, T S. 1970. *An Eighteenth-Century Shopkeeper. Abraham Dent of Kirby Stephen.* Manchester University Press.

Williams, Alastair (Ed). 2004. *The Vulgar Tongue, Buckish Slang and Pickpocket Eloquence* by Francis Grose. (Originally London. 1785). Summersdale.

Wilson, David K. 2005. *The Southern Strategy; Britain's Conquest of South Carolina and Georgia, 1775-80.* University of South Carolina Press.

Young, Rev George. 1817 (1976). *A History of Whitby and Streoneshalh Abbey; with a Statistical Survey of the Vicinity to the Distance of Twenty-Five Miles.* Whitby.

Online Sources:

1911 Encyclopaedia Britannica Online.

Anne Liese's Fibers and Stuff. www.geocities.com/anne_liese_w/Fibers

Bill Lealman's webpage. www.lealman.fsnet.co.uk/filey. Filey

Bickham, Troy O. N. 2002. "Sympathizing with Sedition? George Washington, the British Press, and British Attitudes during the American War of Independence" in *William and Mary Quarterly* Vol 59, Issue 1. Online in association with The History Cooperative, www.historycooperative.org.

 Bruce Ruiz's website. www.bruceruiz.net.

 Dave King's Genealogy Pages. www.davekinggenealogy.co.uk.

 Gale Digital Collections: British Newspapers 1600-1900. www.gale.cengage.com/DigitalCollections

 Historic Cleveland. www.historic-cleveland,co.uk.

 Journal of Du Roi the Elder 1776-1778, trans Charlotte Epping 1911. University of Pennsylvania. www.archive.org/details/duroitheelderdu00augurich.

 Navy and Marine Living History Association. www.navyandmarine.org

 Maritime History Virtual Archives. Transcripts by Lars Bruzelius. www.bruzelius.info/Nautica/Nautica.htm.

 Measuring Worth. www.measuringworth.com.

 Rev War '75. www.revwar75.com

 Wikipedia. en.wikipedia.org

Acknowledgements

  There are so many people whom I would like to thank for their help. Dr Jerzy Litwin, Director of the Polish Maritime Museum at Gdańsk, for allowing me to see all the *General Carleton* artefacts which are not on public display, and for giving permission for the reproduction of numerous pictures in this book. Dr Waldemar Ossowski for his constant and enthusiastic support, and his patience in dealing with my endless questions. Rosalin Barker, who knows so much about the history of Whitby, for her advice and guidance. Christiane Kroebel, Honorary Librarian & Archivist, and Roger Dalladay, Exhibition Manager, both of the Whitby Literary and Philosophical Society for their support and co-operation. Cliff Thornton, President of the Captain Cook Society, who has been able to bring his knowledge to bear on so many difficult questions I have asked. Susan North, Senior Curator of Textiles and Fashion at the Victoria & Albert Museum, for her generous sharing of her expertise on 18th century clothing. Dr Kathy Abbass, of Rhode Island Marine Archaeology Project, for giving me copies of her many-volumed *magnum opus*. Prof Lawrence Babits of East Carolina University for his wide knowledge and unbounded enthusiasm. David Brandon for his excellent lecture course on *Defending These Shores*. Gale Digital Collections for granting me access to their wonderful on-line archives, an essential resource for historical study. Amy Miller and Liza Verity, both of the National Maritime Museum; Dr John D Broadwater, Chief Archaeologist at NOAA's Office of National Marine Sactuaries; Peter G Smithurst, Senior Curator, Firearms at the Royal Armouries; Sue Constable, Shoe Heritage Officer of the Northampton Museum, and Gavin Dixon of the Horniman Museum. And to the many other friends and correspondents (several of whom are members of the Yahoo 'Whitby Group') who have provided me with information, especially: Margaret Holmes, Yvonne Leck, Dave King, Clive Powell, Bob Sanders, Andrew White, Chris Corner, Andrzej Spychała, Avril Hart, Jill Goodwin, Scott McGregor, Ian Marchant and Marion Dennett. And finally I would like to thank my wife Susan for her patience and support: she has not only read through the text pointing out errors and suggesting improvements, but has had to put up with a litter of scattered books and papers.

Illustrations

The following illustrations appear here by kind permission of the Polish Maritime Museum (*Centralne Muzeum Morskie*), Gdańsk:

Line drawings: Figs 2a, 2b, 5a, 5b, 6, 9, 11.
Photographs by B. Galus: 3, 4, 5, 6, 11, 12, 14, 32, 33, 34, 35, 36, 37, 38, 39.
Photographs by E. Meksiak: 15, 24, 25, 26, 27.
Photographs by W. Ossowski: 7, 8, 13, 23, 40.
Photograph L. Nowicz: 9.
Photograph by S. Baines: 2.

The following are etchings by Harvey Taylor, specially created for this book:
Figs 1, 3, 4, 7, 8, 10, 12, 14, 17, 18.

Photographs by S. Baines:
1, 10, 16, 17, 18, 19, 20, 21, 22, 28, 30, 31, 41, 42.

29 is from the author's collection.

INDEX

160

Holmes, John, 32
Holt, Elizabeth, 148
Holt, family, 116, 148
Holt, Jane, 30, 34, 118, 148
Holt, John (1718-1783), 30, 31, 34, 35, 41, 42, 55, 99, 135
Holt, John (1742-1828), 43, 49, 53, 76, 82, 139
Holt, Joseph (1686-1744), 30, 36, 148
Holt, Joseph (1751-1814), 49, 105, 106, 118
Holt, Margaret, 34
Holt, Martha, 35, 43, 46, 58, 141
Holt, Robert, 88
Holt, Thomas (1722-1782), 30, 31, 49, 73, 82, 105, 142
Holt, Thomas (1751-1810), 52, 66
Holt, William, 49, 55
Hope, 31
Hopewell, 28, 29, 30, 36, 109
Hopkins, 67
Hornby, Isaac, 66, 82, 139
Hornby, Thomas, 82, 110, 122, 123, 139
Howe, General, 49, 81
Hudson, Robert, 73
Hudspeth, Anne, 30
Hudspeth, Robert, 30
Hugill, Henry, 36
Hull, 35, 44, 67, 70, 72, 74, 75, 76, 77, 82, 83, 84, 86, 87, 89, 92, 95, 98, 106, 114, 133, 136, 140, 141
Hunter, 47, 81, 106
Hunter, Robert, 58
Hunter, Thomas, 102
Hunter, W, 47
Huntrodes, John, 58
Huntrodes, Thomas, 58
Huntrods, Elizabeth, 118
Hustler, Christopher, 109
Hustler, Jane, 109, 130
Hustler, William (1738-1785), 1, 2, 3, 11, 12, 44, 48, 85, 101, 103, 104, 109, 111, 114, 115, 118, 119, 120, 124, 125, 128, 129, 130, 139, 143, 148, 149, 150
Hustler, William (1738-1801), 42, 52, 130, 143, 148
Hutchinson, John, 70, 139
Hutchinson, Thomas, 42, 52
Hydra, 114

Independence, 105
Industry, 75
Isabella, 42, 73
Isis, HMS, 51
Ismay, George, 86
Israel, Ann, 118

Jackson, Charles, 105, 109
Jackson, J, 48
Jackson, John, 106
Jackson, Ralph, 24, 27, 28, 30, 31, 34, 45, 142
Jakimowicz, B, 14
James and John, 49
James and Mary, 86
James and William, 44, 49
Jane, 45, 85, 92
Jason, 87, 118, 133, 137
Jatkin, Nathaniel, 30
Jefferson, Alice, 142
Jefferson, Anthony, 23, 28, 31, 34
Jefferson, Eleanor, 24, 152
Jefferson, Elizabeth, 23, 30, 135
Jefferson, Jane, 23, 30
Jefferson, John, 23, 24, 28
Jefferson, Nathaniel, 23
Jefferson, Sarah, 66
Jefferson, William, 23, 24, 30, 73
Jenny, 31, 87
John, 31, 138
John and Dorothy, 141
John and Elizabeth, 31, 33, 73
John Swan, 118, 128, 142, 150
Johnson, John, 2, 82, 96, 103, 110, 118, 1?, 139, 150
Johnson, Robert, 88
Johnson, William, 96, 115, 139
Jones, John Paul, 84, 88, 89, 90, 93
Joseph and Hannah, 150
Juno, 50, 74

Kaszubski Brzeg, 13, 14, 0, 128
Kildill, John, 36
Kirby Stephen, 68
Knaggs, John, 74, 100
Knaggs, Richard, 31, 34
Kneeshaw, Joshua, 48, 109

Lacy family, 44
Lacy, Jonathan, 58, 102, 148
Landsort, 1
Langborne, Ann, 43
Langborne, George, 41, 44, 55, 75
Langborne, Nathaniel, 43, 52, 75, 133
Lark, 142
Laurel, 49, 99
Lee, Thomas, 119, 139
Lenox, HMS, 106
Leslie, Capt Patrick, 111
Leviathan, 31
Liberty, 49, 144
Liberty and Property, 121
Linskill, Mr, 58
Linskill, William, 27
Linton, James, 31
Littlefair, George, 80, 81, 96, 139
Lively, 47
London, 1, 2, 21, 28, 29, 31, 32, 36, 42, 44,
45, 48, 49, 52, 54, 65, 67, 70, 72, 73, 74, 75,
77, 82, 84, 87, 91, 95, 101, 103, 104, 106,
109, 110, 114, 115, 116, 118, 119, 123, 128,
129, 130, 133, 135, 136, 137, 138, 139, 140,
141, 142, 143, 144, 149, 150, 157
London Chronicle, 86
Lord Howe, 49, 95, 106
Lord Mulgrave, 106, 108, 109
Lord Sandwich, 85, 91, 99
Lotherington, Benjamin, 31, 102
Lotherington, Mary, 148
Lotherington, Thomas, 31, 49, 102
Love and Unity, 48
Loyal Club, 86
Lyde, 31, 49, 135, 137
Lythe, 27, 28, 47, 136, 137, 141, 144
Lyon, 31

Mackerel, 44, 52, 138
Mackie, James, 111, 140
Malson, Lancelot, 129, 140
Margaret and Martha, 46
Mariner, Magnus, 106
Marlborough, 86, 102, 103, 138, 140
Marshall, James, 23
Marshall, John, 23
Marshall, Robert, 56
Marshall, Thomas, 108

Martha, 49, 53, 54, 55, 116, 133, 150
Martin, William, 73
Marton, William, 111, 114, 140
Mary, 29, 42, 84, 139
Mary and Jane, 23
Mary Ann, 136
Mayflower, 23
Mellar, John, 45
Memel, 44, 74, 75, 76, 106, 129, 133
Mentor, 138
Middleton, Sarah, 133
Middleton, Thomas, 76
Midsummer Blossom, 23, 34, 73, 136
Millner family, 53
Millner, Thomas, 42, 53, 55, 65, 135
Milvil, James, 109
Minerva, 49, 136
Moor, Andrew, 114, 118, 119, 128, 140
Moor, Samuel, 140
Moore, Benjamin, 129, 140
Morrey, George, 111, 140
Myrtle, 136, 150

Narva, 74, 87, 118
Nautilus, 73, 138
Navy Board, 28, 36, 42, 47, 48, 49, 51, 52,
57, 95, 99, 100, 107, 110, 115, 146, 147
Neale, Richard, 2, 112, 114, 118, 140
Nelly, 23, 88
Nelly's Increase, 23
Nelson, 72, 113
New York, 49, 85, 99, 100, 102, 105, 106,
107, 108, 111, 114, 115
Newbegin, 144
Newcastle, 23, 24, 28, 29, 30, 36, 42, 44, 45,
53, 67, 72, 73, 75, 87, 88, 141, 146
Nicholson, John, 118, 119, 128, 140
Nicol, John, 93
Nixon, James, 95, 98, 100, 140
Noble, Andrew, 129, 140
Noble, John, 2, 3, 96, 97, 110, 118, 140
Noble, T, 81
Noddings, Charles, 29, 66, 140
Noddings, Hannah, 66
Noddings, John, 29, 66, 68, 69, 81, 110, 140
North, Susan, 21, 35
Norway, 31, 44, 45, 75, 82, 98, 118, 119,
129, 130